YOUR BUSINESS

THE RIGHT WAY TO RUN IT

YOUR BUSINESS

THE RIGHT WAY TO RUN IT

(THE COMPLETE GUIDE – ESPECIALLY FOR THE BEGINNER)

by

A. G. Elliot

and

A. Clive Elliot

PAPERFRONTS

ELLIOT RIGHT WAY BOOKS
LOWER KINGSWOOD
TADWORTH, SURREY, U.K.

Set, printed and bound in Great Britain by
Cox & Wyman Ltd, Reading

CONTENTS

5

1

THE IMPORTANCE OF POLICY

On the River Clyde in Scotland, before Nationalization was even thought of, they used to build the finest ships in the world. 'Clyde built' stood for the tops in quality. I was once invited to the launching of a liner and, at the point where it was to take place, the river was little wider than the giant ship poised on the bank at a steep angle, ready to plunge into it.

'George,' I said to my engineering companion. 'How will they prevent the ship from shooting across and hitting the opposite bank?'

'There is no danger,' my friend explained. 'The shipyard has fixed numerous chains and other devices to prevent that happening.'

'Suppose one of the chains broke?' I enquired, being doubtful.

'Don't worry,' my friend confirmed. 'Because the shipbuilders work out scientifically the amount required for safety and then *multiply by fifteen times* to make sure that nothing will go wrong.'

What has all this got to do with you? Just this. You, too, may be thinking of launching out. You may be about to become the one who takes all the risks. Remember the Clyde and its fifteen times safety margin, which helped to bring the Clyde shipbuilders profit and fame in their great days.

It is true that if you weighed up every possible happening, few decisions would ever be reached, because all kinds of unlikely things can occur to bring disaster. So you have to draw a line between optimism and pessimism but an excess of the latter is useless. Optimists usually get the best out of life. It is perhaps a good philosophy to remember that the thing we fear most often never happens. It is the unexpected which no-one could foresee which usually brings success or failure. In Britain today, this can most often be some new action or interference by the Government, which can bring instant ruin. Private enterprise must accept such risks.

Capital Needs

More small businesses must have disintegrated for lack of capital than for any other reason. Anyone contemplating opening a business should therefore make a pessimistic estimate of all possible money needs and then add 60% to it to allow for inflation or unexpected disaster and to be reasonably safe. It is madness to run out of capital in the first year or so, because at that time you will not have established goodwill and are, therefore, liable to be sued in Court if you delay paying accounts. Suppliers are rightly suspicious of the new firm, because they know from experience that the percentage of business failures in the early years is high. Later on, it might be possible to get extended credit especially if expansion was contemplated.

I cannot estimate the capital you require, because you would need little if you were going to begin as a window-cleaner operating from your home. On the other hand, if you intend to set up a shop in the high street, considerable capital is necessary.

In the old days, it was possible to save out of income enough capital to start up a business. With the present high tax rates which exist throughout most of the world, that method is less often possible today (though some people get a lot of 'redundancy' money). In any case, it is neither a quick nor an easy method. For this reason, many highly successful businesses have been largely or entirely launched on borrowed money or subscribed share capital.

How much, and whom to borrow from, are the next questions. If the amounts needed are small and you have affluent relatives with confidence in you, there is probably no easier way to acquire capital than to borrow it from them. In your own interest, however, I would say it is folly either:

(*a*) to borrow all from one person unless the sum is but a small proportion of his wealth, or

(*b*) to borrow more than, say, 10% of what the lender is worth.

To illustrate the first point, should you borrow the lot from one individual, you may face disaster if anything happens to him. Under the second heading, if you borrow too large a percentage of someone's capital, the same thing can apply. Or else the lender may try to interfere with the management of your business and thereby jeopardize its future. It is therefore better to borrow from perhaps a dozen people. You must try to spread your risk of trouble.

Banks

In thinking of banks most of us in England picture 'the big 4'. Barclays, National Westminster, Lloyds and Midland, known as the Clearing Banks.

While the main source of profit for banks may be from interest on their loans or overdrafts, one of their chief functions is to act as clearing houses for the transmission of money at home or abroad, look after customers' deposits and other services.

There can be no question that the standard of service provided by banks has deteriorated in recent years. I believe this is because a near-monopoly has been allowed to arise as Governments allowed amalgamations, for example, the National Provincial and the Westminster Banks. The public suffers. It would occupy too much space to explain all my reasons for this view but they are based on over 50 years of being a customer of many branches of what are now 'the big 4'. Competition has diminished and in some areas people have little choice. The Banks have collectively decided not to open on Saturdays, which is the day many people want to use them.

Overdraft Facilities

It is said that banks will grant you overdrafts when you don't need money and not a penny if you do. How true! But in fairness one has to allow for the argument that they must protect their shareholders' and depositors' money. They don't exist to provide 'risk' capital.

By far the cheapest way to borrow money normally is by an overdraft and if a businessman is likely to need cash seasonally or for some special purpose, for example paying income tax or a new plant purchase, it is wise to see the bank manager and discuss the proposition. Estimate weeks ahead the maximum amount you may require and the duration; for example £3,000 needed in about 2 months and for maybe 10 weeks before it can be largely cleared. The reason an overdraft is cheaper is that one pays interest only on the amounts outstanding daily. Unless you arrange it otherwise, your bank may charge you a small amount of interest for retaining your overdraft 'facility'. Don't let them. That soon mounts up.

Before agreeing to grant you an overdraft limit the manager could have to consult Head Office or a regional office, but for small amounts this may not be necessary. The small branch manager probably has a discretionary lending limit of £500, while a large branch manager might be allowed to grant £10,000 on his own. Bankers are human and like most humans, childish, and they prefer everything to be negotiated through them. With exceptions, the managers thus have enormous power which, as always, tends to go to the head, so if one is dependent on their help, discretion may often be the better part of valour.

In my life I have had many arguments because I would never be beholden, either to managers or even area directors. Not a few bankers have been politely informed that my pound is worth exactly the same as the pound of any well-known Public Company, and to remember that I am the customer with the power to remove my account. But then I have never tried to borrow more than I could cover with assets outside my business.

Allow time for negotiations because a favourite bankers' trick is deliberate delay which if you are really short of money increases his power over you. Ask for, say, a 50% higher limit than you need, then if you are squeezed downwards, you may yet have enough.

Facts of Banking Life

We hear of 'hard-faced' bankers. Remember their training and background tend to make them hard. We must remember most of them are second rate today and this in my view is because for decades bank policy was one of not paying adequate salaries, combined with over-strict discipline and unfair 'rules'. It is not that long since a bank clerk had to get 'permission' to marry if under 30. Result? Few good men would touch a bank job but there were exceptions. For example, I walked into one bank, off the street, after a row with another bank manager and this new bank, without seeing any documents, granted me the £4,000 I sought that day for a deal. On another occasion we ran into trouble with a bank head office and I rang another bank speaking to the manager whom I had never met. We only needed a few thousand, but his reply was 'Up to £10,000 now, if you want more talk again.'

So, if you ever run into a neurotic or stupid manager don't be afraid to seek a good one. They still exist. You may have to go far afield to find one, but don't worry as managers can arrange for you to use your nearest branch for paying in or cashing cheques.

Don't expect a bank to grant an overdraft to a new business with no assets. It is another matter if you have a house, shares or insurance policies, etc., but probably you will be lucky if you can borrow a fifth of your total assets. Banks play safe, very safe with new customers. As the evidence of the mid 1970's proved they don't play it safe with all customers; remember how they lent far too much for property deals, etc. If bankers were wiser, in my view, they would depend less on security (or collateral) and more on the guts and integrity of the borrower.

Banks don't expect overdrafts to be permanent. For long term they prefer to lend you a given sum for a period of, say, 3 years, against security, but this is normally at a higher rate of interest and a most costly way of borrowing because the interest accumulates on the *full* sum all the time.

Bankers like active accounts and normally it is easier to get an overdraft for a special reason, for instance building up Christmas stocks, or in farming near the time when crop payments should start, so that the overdraft reduces quickly.

Follow this procedure if you want to try for an overdraft:

1. Never lie or mislead your bank. This does not mean you need blurt out everything or exaggerate the risks – as my mother used to say – 'You need enough o' the de'il in ye to keep the de'il off ye.'

2. If humanly possible, never promise a bank anything to a fixed date. They 'mark your account'. If you have said 'I will clear this overdraft in 60 days' and you have failed, the manager will, rightly, hold that against you. Qualify repayment promises by words such as 'We will expect to have reduced the overdraft by the year end.'

3. Managers are human and like to be treated with respect; so unless you are rich it may not pay you to be too rough with them!

4. Explain fully why you need the money, give them facts and figures and you may be surprised how well they look after you. So much depends, alas, on whether the banks are looking for business or under a government squeeze at the time.

5. Be sure to arrange the interest rate. It is usually between 1% and 2% or 3% over base rate but I hate to say this, bankers, like so many today have become greedy. If you don't ask, they may try and grab 5% over base rate as I found one of the big four

trying on with me. He lost a beautiful overdraft! At the moment
we are paying 2% over base which is far too much considering
that at other times we often have thousands lying idle in the
current account. Watch your bank doesn't pile on the 'charges'.
Compare notes with other business colleagues.

The Secret of Winning

It may happen you have a new branch opening near you. If you
need money go there. Managers at such branches are usually good
and seeking to win new business from their competitors. You
could get more help than from your other bank with a doddering
old manager nearing retirement, who can't be bothered. Banks
promote men who would be retired to grass in any really competitive business. I know because I have met many managers of
quite large branches who are mere commercial idiots.

Collateral

If your bank trusts you, you should be able to arrange security
against an overdraft cheaply. In the old days, banks expected a
house or shop, etc., to be 'made over' to them but this costs
money. They ought to be delighted to take a letter from you
assuring them you will leave the documents, title deeds, land
registry or what, with them in their vaults for safe custody while
the overdraft lasts. Be sure to get a receipt for the safe custody
of your documents. Need I add that even if you have no overdrafts,
you ought to keep important papers, such as wills, title deeds,
insurance policies in the bank safe. Keep copies at home.

Bankers Change, Beware

Early in your business life you should learn that banks often
change their managers, so the decent chap who helped you, may
be promoted one fine day, and the new man is a so-and-so.
He throws his weight about and can hit you hard, unless you are
equally ready. No use saying it does not happen because I have
had letters from more than one chairman or director of the 'big
four', apologizing for the manner in which their men have treated
me. Normally there is little point in complaining 'higher up'
because Head Office usually backs the manager. It may however
prevent the manager treating some other customer badly. The
secret is have two banks. Share your business with them and if

one kicks you, you have the competition. The mere fact that they know you have another bank, often helps to prevent trouble. Banks don't like this and it may well not be easy for you to arrange a second bank. At least try and keep your private account separately or your wife's (or husband's) account which will give you an entrée to the manager. Banks love old and honoured customers and if your wife's account has been satisfactory for 10 years, that means a lot to a manager considering whether to take your account.

The use of computers is the curse of modern business, so be sure you check all bank statements with your ledgers. In the last few years I have found many errors, the largest being £13,000 debited to our account when it ought to have been another Elliot. Computers are only as good as those who feed them and if you look around you, these days, you can see how careless the majority of people are.

The Merchant Banks

Britain probably has the safest clearing banks in the world and she may well have some of the finest Merchant Banks. The men who run them are often superb and the best could be described as the cream of bankers.

These banks find money for large or medium sized firms but are probably of little use to the small company whose turnover is under £100,000. I remember once putting up a proposition to one of these banks for half a million or so. I was ushered into the parlour and we chatted about all sorts of things, but little about the proposition. I am a publisher and I was asked only one question. 'May we ask W. H. Smith & Son about you?' I agreed. A day or two later I had a 'phone call saying the loan could be granted. The snag was they wanted a large proportion of our shares which we were not prepared to give as in time we could have lost control of our Company. We felt this too large a price to pay.

Starting on Credit

Another way of starting a business is to do so on credit. A few have succeeded, but more have failed. It is more difficult than it used to be to obtain extended credit, because of the high cost of borrowing money. The method is to get your various suppliers to extend to you credit of, say, 4 or 6 months.

If you then market their goods for cash or early payment, you can in effect use their money to pay your rates, live on, or pay other essential suppliers who will not give long credit. In theory, this should be possible, because by the end of the fourth or sixth month, your returns, which should include your profits, ought to suffice also to pay the original long credit debts.

In practice, skating on such thin ice usually ends in immersion! It is the old story of no reserves for the unexpected, and the unexpected often happens. It is in fact a method only possible in the kind of trade where very quick turnover is the rule.

To summarize, relations are probably your best chance of raising capital; next are old friends and business associates who have faith in you. Finally, there are banks of one kind or another. If you adopt the method of borrowing from individuals, consult a lawyer and have an agreement. The lenders will expect yearly interest on their money, roughly equivalent to what a bank would charge. Contact your accountant or local tax office for details of what to do tax-wise. If you are starting up as a limited company, you will need to have an accountant anyway, and probably a solicitor's help will be needed to bring the company into being.

Bank overdraft interest rates vary and British rates in recent years have been as low as 6% and as high as 20% at times. There is, of course, a very big difference between these two rates. If you start a business when overdraft interest rates are high, and you have to pay, say, between 10% and 15% for the capital, this makes it more difficult for you to earn a living.

The Time to Start

My fellow countryman, Andrew Carnegie, indicated the time to start a business with these famous words (which made him a fortune of about £40 million), 'Buy during slump.' I may remind you briefly of his career when I say that his fortune was based on buying steelworks in America during a slump when they could be purchased below their market value. It is usually good to start any business when costs are low, so that less capital is required. One must not, however, place too much reliance on timing, because the many exceptions prove that success can follow even when businesses have started at what might be called the wrong moment.

Good times generally follow bad. If you had the courage to

start in a slump, when you get in 'on the ground floor' as the saying is, you could be lucky.

Where to Start Your Business

Certain types of business, such as shipping agents, agricultural merchants and so on, must be situated in the area where there is a demand. That is to say, for the first mentioned (normally) in a sea port, while agricultural merchants would not probably do very well in the middle of a large city.

But many businesses have considerable choice in their area of operation. This needs thought. It would indeed be a bold and probably foolish man who opened a cut-price clothing store next to Marks and Spencer's. Among the matters to be thought of are such items as:

(1) Where is the cheapest place to start? (Time is money, and travelling uses energy. Try to work near your home.)

(2) Is the business you contemplate in an area where the population is decreasing, or are you in an expanding town? There is a lot to be said for coming in on the crest of a wave.

(3) If your business depends on a passing trade, is there sufficient? Is there any danger of the road being diverted, or of a new development which will take all the shoppers to the other end of town?

(4) Have you too many competitors near you, or can you specialize so as to make use of the fact that there are competitors who will bring customers into the neighbourhood?

(5) Are you near a bank and post office?

(6) Are you in the right area for supplies?

The above are the kind of points to consider.

2

ORGANIZATION PREMISES AND EQUIPMENT

Organization

There are three basic types of business organization that are common in the United Kingdom today, the sole trader or partnership, the private company, and the public company.

The Sole Trader or Partnership

The sole trader covers every category of self-employed person, who is in business on his own account. The enterprise can be anything from a one-man window-cleaner to a small shop employing perhaps a number of people.

The important thing to remember is that the proprietor is himself personally responsible for all his debts. This means that if the enterprise fails, he may have to sell his home, his car, indeed everything except the clothes he stands up in and the tools of his trade. Where a sole trader's liabilities exceed his assets, he can be adjudged bankrupt.

A partnership is a form of association between two or more people who get together for business purposes. This is quite common in small enterprises, and is also the appropriate form of organization for groups of such professional people as doctors, architects, solicitors or stockbrokers. The point about ordinary partnerships is that the liability of each partner is unlimited, so that each can be separately held responsible for the entire debts of the partnership. It is, however, possible to set up a limited partnership in which the liability of *some*, but not all of the partners, is limited to the amount they have subscribed.

When forming a partnership, it is particularly important to make proper provision in the deed for what is to happen in the event of the death or resignation of one of the partners. If this is not satisfactorily sorted out at the start, it may be impossible for the other partner or partners to continue the business.

There are two principal disadvantages to partnerships, which apply particularly where the enterprise grows. The first is, the unlimited nature of the liability on the part of each partner. The second is the impossibility of raising capital for expansion. Partnerships in the U.K. cannot set aside money out of past profits for future expansion, except after such profits have been fully taxed in the partners' own hands as individuals. This, therefore, leads us on to the next form of organization, which is the private company.

Private Companies

The limited liability, private company or something similar is the basis of the private enterprise system in all capitalist countries. Virtually all the great industrial giants that exist in the world today started at one time as a small private company of one kind or another. Within living memory Marks & Spencer has grown from a penny stall in a street market.

This differs very much from the partnership or sole trader, in that the liability of the shareholders is limited to the amount that they have paid for the shares they own. The normal procedure for setting up a company is for each shareholder to subscribe a sum of money and buy shares in the company. The money thus received by the company becomes the basic capital of the company. This money can then be used to buy premises, plant, equipment and stock, etc., and enables the company to start in business.

One advantage of the private, limited company is that it enables other people (i.e. people who are not actually going to be involved themselves in the running of the company) to subscribe money to the company, and to receive pay-off in the form of dividends if the company is profitable. This may open up good possibilities of raising capital from relations or outsiders.

Another advantage of the private company is that it becomes possible to a certain extent to set aside money out of previous profits for future expansion. Owing to the tax laws, this can only be done to a limited extent in the U.K., but it is still useful.

A third advantage of the private company is that participants can sell their shareholding to the other participants, or perhaps to new people, if they require their money back for some reason. The same applies in the event of the death of a shareholder.

In Britain, it is a sad fact that shares in private companies are treated as though they were cash in the hands of the owner, and for this reason it can become impossible for a private company to continue under the same family's ownership upon the death of a large shareholder. This applies, of course, mainly to the large kind of company, but it is fair to say that any company worth over £100,000 may not be able to continue in business upon the death of a major shareholder. Except in unusual circumstances it will have to be sold to meet the tax bill.

There is also another form of private company called the unlimited company. This is very rare and differs from the private, limited company in two main ways. Firstly, the liability of each shareholder is unlimited, as in a partnership. Secondly, the private unlimited company is not obliged to submit details of its accounts for public inspection at Companies House. For this reason, the unlimited company status is normally only used by companies which are small but extremely successful, so that there is no danger of bankruptcy or liquidation, but also so that suppliers, customers and competitors are unable to discover just how well the company is doing. This can be useful where the company is dependent on one large customer or one large supplier, or where it has secret processes or methods of which it wishes to conceal the value.

The Public Company

This status is appropriate for large enterprises (in the U.K., generally with profits well over £250,000). Shares in public companies are quoted on the Stock Exchange, and can be bought and sold by members of the public, through stockbrokers. For this reason, the rules require extremely wide disclosure of material particulars such as capital, profits, and trading success or failure. Sometimes a private company becames so large and successful that it wishes to become a public company. In the U.K., this is arranged through merchant banks and stockbrokers, and is called a 'flotation' or a 'placement'.

A company, whether it is a private or a public one, has to give an annual statement of accounts to its shareholders. These accounts are checked by an auditor, who is a member of an approved body of accountants, and he certifies that the figures do present a true and accurate picture of the company's performance during the year under review. Even the smallest private company must have its figures audited in this way.

How to Start

If you are starting from scratch, you will either work as sole proprietor, or you will form a private, limited company. If the form of enterprise is one in which you are offering a service, as it were, on a free-lance basis, and you do not need to involve your own capital to any great extent, then my advice is to start as a sole trader or partnership. On the other hand, if you are going to have to buy or rent premises and buy stock and equipment, then you might be better to form a private, limited company, so that you are not liable to be rendered personally bankrupt, in the event of things going wrong.

Economy

William Morris, the motor manufacturer, started in a bicycle shop, but fifty years later Morris cars were used the world over. This book is not written for millionaires, but for those with a thousand pounds or two. I speak from personal experience in saying that when you start a business, your capital may run away so quickly that you will wonder where it went. I make no excuse for urging that the small businessman, unless he is lucky, will have to watch even the pence he spends for months, or probably for years. In a struggling, new business, you will need to use improvisation and 'make do and mend' methods, which later you may abandon. I expect that, until recently, the only money you controlled was your weekly or monthly pay, apart from some money which I hope you were able to save or were lucky enough to inherit.

As the owner of a business, you will not have someone handing you so much every week, but if you have £1,000 in the Bank, the lot can be drawn out by signing a cheque. It gives the average man a rich feeling to think that he has five hundred pounds in his wallet instead of his usual fifty pounds. The temptation to spend it, to those who are not trained in handling and carrying money, is immense. Your motto should, therefore, be, 'I must not spend it just because I have it.'

Capital is to your business what blood is to your body. You cannot exist without it. This capital will act as your reserve strength on the wrong days when business is bad, or perhaps when you are ill and unable to work. The new businessman must watch his expenditure all the time.

Equipment

That beautiful typewriter or adding machine you want to buy may be what you need, but for now you have got to be content with the old second-hand one. I know that economy can be carried too far, but I can assure you that few businesses finish up in the receiver's hand because of that. More often the reverse.

At times, money must be spent to obtain or to hold business. I will deal with that later. However, the beautiful desk with its 'essential' drawers is not for you; anyway, not yet. Equipment you buy, such as typewriters, intercoms, etc., will not impress the bank. If you hit hard times, second-hand goods have little value. Your bank manager is far more likely to be impressed if you can show him good pending orders or signed contracts for jobs in hand. Here I am assuming that you have either got an office or premises of some sort, but of course in many types of business there may be no need for this expenditure yet.

The small business, whatever number of people are employed, needs to provide them with suitable accommodation, desks or benches, as the case may be. At the risk of being accused of contradicting my own remarks on economy, I must stress the importance of adequate space light and heat, even if it means putting extra windows or radiators into existing buildings. Building and heating extras are costly, though less so if you can find a local retired man with previous experience who will do the job for a small sum. Minimum standards are laid down for the U.K. in the Offices, Shops and Railway Premises Act as regards the temperature, ventilation and lighting, the amount of air space per person, sanitary and washing facilities, fire precautions and first-aid items which must be kept. In any case, it is false economy to have too many people working in cramped, ill-ventilated conditions. Give thought to this question to suit your particular needs.

Nearly every business requires a telephone, though such a luxury as a telegraphic address and the possession of various codes may not be necessary at this stage. Perhaps you are expecting me to recommend that you lay in a stock of such items as filing cabinets, card indexes and so on. Here is where you can practise economy. The most modern business advisers now tend to favour more simple methods.

I remember years ago when I was in a giant business, we used to file every letter we received. Today, I consign about 98% of them to a giant waste-paper basket. I have been doing so for years and have since been joined in this policy by one or two world-famous concerns. These firms have at last discovered that a tremendous amount of time and money can be saved by filing only important papers or those which may have to be referred to later. 'In competitive business, profit is nothing more or less than a commission on economy,' to quote my friend, the late Sir Ernest Benn. This does not mean that you can allow the office boy to decide what to file and what to throw away, but so long as you do it yourself, or employ people of intelligence to do it, there is no need to keep every unimportant letter which is received. In this way, you save time, money and space for filing cabinets. Space costs a lot, both to rent and heat. In my business we now use only small alphabetical, extending Manilla files. We have thousands of letters, but so few are important that one file lasts a couple of years.

Here is what you must keep, as an absolute minimum:

(1) Proper records of account, to show how much people owe you, and a proper system for chasing up slow payers.

(2) Proper records to show how much you have paid out, including a petty cash book for small cash items. Remember that all business expenditure is allowable against your tax liability.

(3) In the U.K. you must keep proper records of your V.A.T. inputs and outputs (if you are registered) so that you can account for V.A.T. correctly to the Revenue Authorities.

(4) You are required to keep proper records of the amount of money paid to your employees, and to account for the National Insurance Contributions and Tax paid to the Inland Revenue.

Big business can cope with the need to keep records in very sophisticated ways. The biggest firms probably use computers for their accounts and writing cheques, for paying the wages, for keeping track of their stocks, etc. Even a medium sized business can probably benefit greatly from some mechanization of its accounting procedure. For you, however, with a new business, all of this is a luxury which you cannot afford. All you are going to have is a couple of Manilla files, an ordinary ledger, a bank book, and a P.A.Y.E. file and other materials issued by the Inland Revenue. The other essentials for running a normal business are probably just a book of order forms, some headed notepaper, and a book to write down how much you pay into the bank and the cheques you draw. Don't go investing in expensive systems until you can see how the business is going.

Correspondence Files

You have to be able to find the 2% of letters which *are* important. You must be able to refer to contracts you have made, to prices that you have quoted, and to a few other essential items. What I do is to keep all important letters in a small Manilla foolscap file which can be bought for only a pound or two. Each section is headed with a letter of the alphabet.

In industry, much thought has been given to time and motion study and methods of labour saving in manufacturing. It is only recently that consideration has been given to similar methods in office organization and clerical routines.

All round my desk, I have some one hundred pigeon-holes, a large number of which can be reached without leaving my chair. These are simply made from small uprights of timber with hardboard shelves and the pigeon-holes are separated by ordinary thin wire. I cannot tell you how useful they are. Any businessman will be wise to see that his staff have lots of pigeon-holes around them to save them walking about too much and opening drawers. This depletes their energy.

A desk with sufficient drawers will do instead of pigeon-holes. Looking at my pigeon-holes as I write this, I find within reach of my hand, nine pigeon-holes, one for each of our U.K. representatives, another pigeon-hole for accounts, another one for stock records, another one for quotations, then there is one for each of our four main printers, one for each of our three biggest customers, ten for manuscripts in the course of production, one for insurance, nine for our overseas agents and representatives, and so on. Everything is at my fingertips, and I can give the answers to a telephone enquiry almost straight away.

Organization

Obviously the amount of organization you have depends on the size of your business. The one-man business in which the owner controls everything requires little, because he keeps in his mind most of the details. This section on organization is essential because the one-man business may become the fifty-man business.

Alternatively, the type of business may require detailed organization, with only a few people, as, for example, the average shop. If you employ a lot of people, things always become more complex. Such matters as how the work is to be divided, how records are to be kept, how the premises are to be heated and insured and so on, although possibly small matters in themselves, are collectively vital. I can only write generally because obviously one business will require one organization and another will need something completely different.

Humble Premises

Unless you live in a rented house, where the legal position may be difficult, many small businesses can start at home until it is discovered whether they are going to progress. You have to be careful about planning restrictions if starting a business at home. Clearly, areas which are zoned as residential cannot be turned into office blocks or factories without permission. Nor can a builder's yard or a boarding kennel be suddenly inserted into a row of terraced houses. The salient point is, are you going to harm the amenities of a district, and is anyone going to notice? I think the answer is that you are safe to start at home provided it is some kind of business which can be suitably operated there. For example, a commercial photographer or a freelance journalist could no doubt do it from his house without anyone being the wiser or making any complaints. On the other hand, a business which spoilt the amenities would be in trouble from such bodies as the District Council and the Residents' Association, and there would be little wisdom in opening up a lot of ill-will against you.

If you are a tenant, the position is delicate and your guiding procedure should be common sense. If in doubt, consult a good solicitor, repeat, a good one. After all, authors, dentists, dressmakers, typewriting agencies and so on frequently run from home without complaint.

I do not visualize operating from home as being anything of a permanent nature. I merely put in the suggestion as one of economy, until you see whether this particular business is going to last and win.

Rent or Buy?

On the assumption that you must have business premises, your aim should be to try to find something inexpensive, yet suitable. It will probably pay you to rent premises, or a part of premises, rather than to buy. Yes, the desire to own is strong. But it is often costly. It is true that banks may be willing to lend money against business property, but at this stage when you are likely to be poor, it is normally wiser to pay rent. After all, as far as the U.K. is concerned the rent of your building, office, shop or warehouse is chargeable as an expense against profits. If you buy premises, this is capital expenditure, and such a charge will not be permitted. (The position is different if the business is a factory.) If possible, avoid tying up capital in premises.

I urge the importance of having an escape clause in your lease, or, if need be, several breaks, regarding ending your agreement to pay rent so that, if, by chance, your business fails, you will not be saddled with responsibility for it. However, by the same token, property owners invariably insert review clauses into leases, so that they can increase the rent at a fixed date later on. If you are renting, find out whether the rent includes rates, repairs, etc., or whether you are responsible for such items. In short, find out what you are getting for the rent and what other items you will be responsible for. Rather than spending precious capital, it is sometimes possible to obtain premises by buying them on a mortgage. This applies particularly to such things as shops with living quarters above, and in these circumstances it is wise to raise the money by a mortgage if possible. By buying on a mortgage you preserve much of your capital, and, with inflation, you repay in money of depreciating value. Although the availability of mortgage loans varies enormously from time to time, it is at times possible to get one for a large percentage of the total at the time of purchase. It is much harder, if not impossible, to get one later. The people to approach for a mortgage or for information are:

> Building Societies
> Insurance Companies
> Insurance Agents or Brokers
> Industrial Banks
> Your Bank Manager

Again, your accountant or solicitor may be able to help, as they may have clients interested in this type of investment or you may personally know an individual who is willing to be the mortgagee. Be sure to get the documents properly drawn up by your solicitor.

One circumstance in which it would be particularly wise to buy your premises rather than to rent them, is if yours is the type of business which only requires money at certain seasons of the year. It is normally possible to borrow easily from banks against the security of 'bricks and mortar'. If yours is this kind of business, it might be better only to pay interest during the 'borrowing season' rather than to have unused cash resources lying about for the rest of the year.

The Early Days

The most difficult period is the first few months or years. Probably few businesses can be described as properly established until they are four or five years old, by which time your accountants should be able to help you to obtain a picture of what is happening. In these early years, until you can get an insight of whether you are making money, breaking even, or losing, it is essential to watch every penny of expenditure so that your capital can be put to its best use. This, of course, depends on the nature of the business. In many businesses, the best use of capital will be well-bought stock, but in other types of business the capital may be required for advertising, wages, or even for raw materials. You can be practically certain that even having allowed for more capital than you anticipated, you will eventually find that you are short of it at times.

Buy a Business or Start from Scratch?

Personally I consider it better to start from scratch. In this way you get the kinds of stocks and organization that you want. However, it is sometimes wiser or essential to buy an established business. Do beware here. There are tricks in all trades, and your best insurance against them is to buy from an honest seller.

Realize that sellers usually want as much as they can get for 'goodwill' as it is called. Goodwill is generally reckoned to be three years or so of profit. A business with £15,000 a year average profit might want £45,000 for the goodwill.

Unfortunately, goodwill is a capital payment and cannot be charged as a cost, tax-wise. From the point of view of the seller, this is an advantage, because he normally gets taxed on his capital gain at a lower rate than he would if it were treated as income, in the U.K. From your point of view as a buyer, it is, however, disadvantageous. It may be possible to reduce the goodwill by some method of retaining the former owner as a partner for a few years and paying him a share of the profits but get legal advice on this. You must retain full control, and be able to get rid of the partner by a certain date, as well as keep within the tax regulations.

3

MONEY AND SYSTEMS

Few businessmen, unless they have had the benefit of a good training or business background, fully realize the importance of dealing with money correctly.

There are many essentials, and vital among them are the following:

(1) Pay your accounts to a system.
(2) Collect your accounts to a system.

Do not under any circumstances deviate from these rules. 'Simple,' you say, 'Of course I will.' You would be surprised if you knew, as I do, how many people crash because they fail under either (1) or (2) of the above.

When you are buying goods, never forget that they have to be paid for. That is obvious, but is not what I meant by 'Pay your accounts to a system'. I meant select a day in the week or month for paying accounts, and make it an absolute rule to do so, or to have a very good reason for not doing so.

Short of Cash?

There may be a time when your finances are stretched, and it could be embarrassing or impossible to pay.

This is the time to lie low and keep your mouth shut. Don't damage your credit by telling anyone of your difficulty, as a few people do. The moment it gets around that you are not meeting payments, creditors are apt to lose confidence and press for payment – the last thing you want.

There is one exception to this. If some of the accounts are marked 'Kindly remit immediately', or if you start getting letters which begin 'Unless . . ., etc.', please, for your own sake, do not ignore them. Act at once. Call, phone, or write in *confidence* to your creditor and explain briefly your position. If you can, re-assure the creditor by telling him that you are expecting some money in a few days, weeks, or even months as the case may be.

Promise that the moment you get the cash in, you will remit. Alternatively, explain that you are waiting on some money and send a payment 'to account'. Even a 20% payment will usually quieten the creditor for a month or two.

Not a Time for Silence

What annoys the normal creditor is silence. He regards it as an insult, which usually it is. All creditors know that the man who is courteous enough to write, or to make a part payment, usually pays in the end.

Why are You In Trouble?

Provided your business started with reasonable capital, any running short of money usually means that something is wrong – probably seriously. Therefore investigate at once. Ask yourself such questions as:

    (a) Am I overtrading?
    (b) Have I bought wrongly?
    (c) Am I paying too high wages?
    (d) Am I spending too much privately? (A common fault.)
    (e) Am I failing to collect my accounts?
    (f) Is my profit margin too low?
    (g) Could I recover my position by selling some items quickly, or am I losing orders?
    (h) Is reorganization necessary?
    (i) Is my capital diminishing because of too many overheads?

Most probably, the cause will not be just one of these, but several.

Act Drastically

If you don't, the situation is likely to become serious unless luck comes to your aid.

Disasters rarely hit those who do something to prevent them. Among the measures, possibly temporary, which you may have to take under these headings are:

    (a) Stop buying.

(*b*) Analyse what you are buying wrongly.

(*c*) Reduce staff, salaries, or shorten the working week.

(*d*) Cut out those parties, drinks, cigarettes, etc.

(*e*) I deal with this fully later in the chapter.

(*f*) Go into your margin of profit, and see if you need to or could increase it.

(*g*) Consider whether a cut-price sale to a large customer could help to get some money in quickly. Or a contract which could turn some of your stocks into cash.

(*h*) Cultivate fishy eyes, and examine all overheads. Consider changing to cheaper premises.

(*i*) Are there some things which could be better performed by yourself or someone else? Are all these jobs necessary anyway? That outside salesman or counter assistant, is he worth keeping?

Or is it that you are doing jobs the office girl could do better, and leave you free for money-making activities? Think of any possible readjustments. Call in your staff and tell them of the seriousness of your position, and ask for money-saving or money-making ideas. They may surprise you!

Paying the Bills

A large business might keep ledgers in which to record details of invoices and statements received. A bigger business still could possibly find it economic to employ a computer. The smaller businessman probably has no use for any of these adjuncts. Remember that computers cost money, and bought ledgers require bought ledger clerks! It does depend on your type of business and its size. Personally, I find a small Manilla file the ideal method. When an invoice arrives, it is checked to make sure that it tallies with the amount and description of goods to which it relates, and that it is correctly priced, and the extensions and addition calculations are correct. Then it is put into the Manilla file under the initial letter of the firm which sent it. When statements arrive, these are put into the file also.

Each Thursday, we go through the file, extracting the invoices which are due for payment and checking the statements. Normally, we return the statement with our remittance to the firm concerned. The invoice is marked 'Paid', with the date, and is then put into a special pigeon-hole to be processed for V.A.T. later.

Towards the end of each month, this pigeon-hole is again gone through, and the invoices for the previous month are entered in the V.A.T. book and are then finally filed away in another alphabetical Manilla file, because they need checking eventually by the accountants.

As far as normal monthly invoices are concerned, these are due for payment at the end of the month following the date of the invoice. In order to save bank charges, we pay very small accounts by postal order.

This system is adequate for quite a large sort of business, and it would be a big enterprise which really needed anything more sophisticated.

Cash Ledgers

In your cash ledger, you must record all payments on the debit side and all money received on the credit side. You may find it much more convenient to have a separate ledger for each type, but in this case you must be very careful not to enter anything in the wrong book. Similarly, you can have a more sophisticated system, under which ledger entries can be subdivided into different categories.

Such ledgers would be legally required by your accountants. It is essential in all your entries to give sufficient detail to enable your accountant to know what is what. This would be particularly so if you were a small business and mixed your business money with your income or personal expenses.

In appendix I (page 115) I give sample entries from our general ledger, showing both an incoming and an outgoing page.

If your business is the kind which receives a lot of cheque payments from different customers, it may be advisable to have a separate book showing how each bank payment is made up. In this way you can check if there is some error, and a customer asserts that he has already paid your account.

Invoice and Sales Ledgers

What oil is to a sheikh, finance is to business. If your finances go wrong, the end is likely to be near. You would be horrified if you knew how many businessmen fail because of inefficiency in this department. Whether you handle your own accounts, or whether you have an assistant to do them for you, the following are the vital points.

Invoices

Make sure that these go out as nearly as possible the same day as the goods are shipped, or as the work is done. Work out a system whereby this cannot be overlooked. The office diary, explained on page 41, could be useful here. Some other rules such as 'All invoices must accompany goods' or 'All invoices to be sent out by the end of each week' will suffice. If you use an order book or pad you may have a method of marking it as items are invoiced.

Few things are more annoying than delayed, missing or inaccurate invoices. In most businesses it is essential to have all invoices checked, and it is wise to make the checkers initial them.

Where amounts are large, and the number of invoices small, it is best for you to check them yourself. You can lose money fast if invoices are wrong. It may suffice to check samples of them now and again, but always check them exhaustively if you have new invoice clerks.

Not all customers are honest. In some trades, dishonesty is such that where a mistake is against you, the recipient of the invoice does not point it out but regards it as a 'win'. I am glad to say that does not apply in either of the trades I have been connected with, timber and book publishing, where a high standard of integrity exists.

Let me recount a couple of experiences which demonstrate the need for accuracy and promptness in the invoicing department.

A small businessman did a job for me valued at about £20. He sent no invoice. Six months later I reminded him. I told him I would send a cheque the moment I had the exact amount. He said it had been overlooked and he would attend to it. A year later I again reminded him but heard no more. Two years later I wrote yet again and asked for the bill. I never got it, so gave up trying. That was sixteen years ago, and soon after that, I heard he had closed down as he could not make a living.

Around the same time, I bought about £50 of mechanical equipment from another firm, and despite four requests for an invoice, it was never received.

If the above two were isolated instances, I would not mention them, but this sort of carelessness is common nowadays.

Time Saving in Invoicing

Depending on the type of business, you may be able to work out a time-saving invoice. For instance, where you are selling a number of different sorts of the same article at the same price, it is not necessary to itemize each sort separately. A brief summary with the total to be charged at the bottom may be all that is needed, e.g.

> three gross red markers,
> three gross green,
> three gross blue,
> three gross black,
> total 12 gross at £10 a gross, £120
> + V.A.T. . . .

Wherever you have operations in your office which are repetitive, try to make a system and have a printed or duplicated form to ease and speed up the work. Such methods also help to eliminate errors, omissions, and work boredom.

Whatever your invoicing system, make sure that it is easy to calculate your liability to Value Added Tax at the end of each quarter, otherwise you could be in serious trouble with the Customs & Excise Authorities.

Credit Notes

In a small business, you may not require a printed Credit Note. You can use a letter-heading or an Invoice form, with the word Invoice scored out, and the words 'Credit Note' added in red. In an invoice where you have the word 'To', it means 'Due to'. In a Credit Note you use the word 'By', in red. It is usual to have the whole of the wording on the Credit Note, including the figures and the extension in red. This avoids confusion. Unfortunately, most computers do not seem to be able to write in red, and they usually put the letters CR after the sum to denote that it is a credit. Watch out for this if you have computerized suppliers.

Statements

Normally your customer will not pay on receipt of the invoice, but will await your statement. Most businesses issue their statements monthly. Especially for the new business, monthly is much better than quarterly, as it gets your money in quickly. At the end of each month, you issue your statements. These are usually made to fit window envelopes, after folding, so as to save addressing the envelope.

Sales Ledger

Any but the very smallest business will probably require a sales ledger, if a substantial proportion of the business is on credit account. In the sales ledger, under each customer's name, you enter the invoice amounts and any details required. From this your monthly statements will be made up.

There are many types of inexpensive ledgers on the market, but you can always make one yourself with an old ledger and some sheets of paper which you can buy at the stationers. (See the Appendix (page 116) for example.) More sophisticated systems include 'visible sheet' ledgers, which speed up the time taken to find the ledger page necessary to make an entry. Quite large businesses will probably employ some sort of mechanized accounting system, and most big businesses seem to believe that it is cheapest to use a computer. Computers are, however, only as intelligent as the people who programme them, if that.

Overdue Accounts

Here is a man-size job; if you can collect these your troubles may end. Collecting them well needs experience and perhaps a gift for it. From long experience, I set down the best methods in what I usually find to be the order of merit.

(1) If the debtor is nearby, call. Take the statement with you. Do not be angry, but try not to be put off. Do your best to get payment or something on account. The man may owe you £500. If you can collect £100 each time you call, that soon helps. If the debtor is a shopkeeper, remember that these people do not like having suppliers standing in their shop demanding money.

(2) If calling yourself or sending one of your staff is not possible, you can use letters. To avoid any risk of libel, however slight, mark both envelope and letter 'Strictly confidential'. If the letter is to a limited company, address the envelope to the Chairman or Managing Director. Otherwise

address it to the Proprietor or one of the Partners. Here are the kind of letters you can send:

First Letter

Dear Sirs,
                              Strictly Confidential

We write to ask if you could please pay our account as shown on the enclosed statement, now three months overdue.

We have many engagements to meet in the coming weeks, and we trust you can let us have a cheque within the next ten days.

                                        Yours faithfully,
                                        . . . .

(If still unpaid) Second Letter
Dear Sirs,
                              Strictly Confidential

It is now fourteen days since our letter to you requesting immediate payment of our account of £   :   p, and we have had no reply. We regret that if we do not receive payment by return, you are leaving us little option but to put the matter in the hands of our solicitors without further notice.

                                        Yours faithfully,
                                        . . . .

By careful wording of the second letter you are not committed to issue a writ, and you can still employ some other method at a later date. Or you can instruct your solicitor to take proceedings. Many people will pay when they get a letter from your solicitor. However, except where large sums are involved, it is not usually worth taking legal proceedings.

Telephone

A 'phone call is sometimes better than a letter. You can often speak to a partner, or a director of the company, or to the firm's accountant if they have one. The advantage is that you frequently may learn something. Debtors are human, and are not always the so-and-sos we imagine.

The conversation can be on the lines of trying to find out what is the cause of the delay and what are the prospects of payment of all or part of the account. It is unwise to lose one's temper, but good if you can get a promise of money by a certain date. This gives you the excuse for another 'phone call or visit if payment is not forthcoming.

If the debtor has no money, and no hope of any, you can write off your loss. But if he has some cash or is expecting some soon, the odds are good that you will get payment of your account in proportion to the amount of will-power you put into your effort to collect it.

The Humorous Approach

Particularly for small, old accounts, I have found it extremely useful to make comments on the statement, once again marking it and the envelope 'Strictly confidential'. I have not found the usual 'Kindly remit' helpful. Far better, in my experience, is the appeal to the heart. You will be surprised at how effective this can be. Here are just a few of my methods 'Oh, dear,

    £......p
    S.O.S.
    P.T.O.'

and then, on the back, 'R.S.V.P. Hurry, wife and two to keep, to say nothing of the dog.'

You can vary this theme endlessly, depending on a variety of things such as who the customer is, how large the sum, how old the account, etc. It is a job calling for skill and not normally to be trusted to low-grade staff, for what happened to me may happen to you. Incredible as this story is, one of my people, trying to help me while I was on holiday, wrote on a statement to Harrods Ltd., Britain's world-renowned store (and a firm who, of course, always pay as due) the following: 'Remit now or P.T.O.' and on the reverse of the statement, 'You're for the big drop.'

The stupid man had dated the statement the year before accidentally, and thought the account was a year old when it was not. Also, being ignorant, he did not realize that Harrods were the great firm they are. This took one of my most diplomatic letters to clear up, but Harrods accepted my explanation and apology with their customary magnanimity.

Last Resorts

Finally, when you are facing the need to take legal action, do not forget that legal action can be expensive. It may cost little to ask your solicitor to write a letter to the defaulter. It costs a great deal more to take out a writ, even the issue of a default summons. Remember that solicitors are in business, as you are, and you pay for their services according to the amount of time you take up. For this reason it is now probably true to say that it is not worth taking out a summons in the U.K. for a debt under £100, and probably nearer £250 would be needed to make it really worthwhile. Even in this case, you would certainly want to be sure that you could prove delivery of the goods, or that the services had been carried out. For this reason, it is usually better for small sums, to offer to settle for, say, three quarters or half of the total 'to save issuing a writ'. Dozens of times I have found this successful, and within months or a year or two, the customer has gone into liquidation. You rarely receive more than a few pence in the pound in a bankruptcy.

Businessmen who are on the verge of insolvency are often decent chaps. Do not bully them. Sympathize with them, and if possible enlist their sympathy for you. If they like you and if you have played the game with them by extending credit or withholding legal action, frequently they will help you when they know they are sunk.

I remember one man who sent me £49 a week before he received a winding-up order and another who, shortly before his bankruptcy, gave £100 worth of goods which I was able to sell against a £105 debt.

Credit Terms

These vary from trade to trade. Tailors almost expect to be kept waiting for months, though they might not like to hear me say it. On the other hand, in the timber and paper trades, where amounts are often large, payment in a strict thirty days is the rule. In my own publishing business, we often extend long credit to trusted customers and we have rarely been let down.

If you have a big account problem, consult a trusted friend, your bank manager, your accountant or your solicitor. The last will probably be most expensive. A good solicitor – hard to find – will generally urge you to keep out of court. A good businessman will usually urge you to keep out of solicitors' hands.

Shall I Give Credit?

Most firms have to give credit. The problem is to know to whom to grant it, for you can lose much by trusting the wrong people.

While it is true that you will have to learn from your own experience, there are some general hints that I can give.

A lot of tiny customers are safer than a smaller number of doubtful, larger ones. You thus spread your risk. One of the secrets is knowing the customer. If Mr. Brown, who has traded in the same premises for years, and owns his own house, comes along with a job for you, you may be wise to trust him even if you know nothing of him personally. Ask yourself such questions as:

> Is he a sober person?
> Is he well dressed?
> Are his premises in good condition?
> Do his staff look well-paid and happy?
> Is he interested in the price or cost of the job?
> Does he own a car?

The man who considers the price carefully usually pays.

Beware of the person who wants everything done regardless of cost, unless you know for certain that he is extremely rich. No-one who has money need object to being asked for a reference or two. Particularly if the sum is large, you should get two trade references and a bank reference. The private or trade references you can write to yourself, but because of etiquette, you must take up the bank reference through your own bank.

To other suppliers, you merely write a polite letter saying the customer has given them as a reference and you would be obliged if they would reply (in the enclosed stamped, self-addressed envelope) if they consider him honourable, and good for the sum of (say, five hundred pounds). Mark the enquiry and envelope '*Confidential*'. Such enquiries are privileged, and anything, so long as it is true, can be said.

Bankers have their own jargon for references. *Certain* or *undoubted for your figure* is very good indeed. Next best is *considered good for your figure and purpose* which would apply to perfectly good customers. Slightly less to be relied upon is '*should prove good*' . . . there could be a small element of risk here. When you get *considered respectable . . . would not enter into commitments he couldn't fulfil*, this looks good but in fact is a bit dodgy. Perhaps he owes a lot of money and the Bank does not want to do anything which could jeopardize his business. *Unable to speak for your figure* means he is no good. Either the Bank is bouncing his cheques or else the account is unused or dormant. If in doubt, consult your own Bank Manager.

Some people may trick you. They may use a few of their associates whom they pay promptly as referees, whereas there may be other suppliers whom they never pay. This is especially true, I regret to say, of people in what is called the third world.

It is often wise also to obtain a reference as to integrity, because sometimes wealthy people are dishonest in other ways and may for instance make unfair or unjustifiable claims upon you.

Some Other Hints

Watch the fellow who buys a small order once or twice and pays promptly, then sends a very large order. He may be all right, or this may be a tricky way of getting goods on credit with no thought of paying.

Where there is doubt, you can use old tried methods:

> Enquire of a friend in the trade.
> Request cash with order.
> Request deposit in advance of, say, half the sum.
> Request cash on delivery (using the Post Office system).
> Request cash against Pro Forma Invoice.

This last simply means that when the goods are ready, or if they have to be specially made, you send an Invoice marked 'PRO FORMA' (with a short letter requesting payment in advance if you feel the person may not know what pro forma means).

In the main your own judgement must be the best guide. One thing which can be checked is a phone number – this is some guarantee that the firm or person is at least permanently at one address. Remember that out-and-out crooks do moonlight flits, and it is not easy to trace them.

Trade Associations often have a credit reference department or can give advice.

There are also specialized firms who may both give credit advice and collect bad debts for you. These are often over-rated, at least as far as their debt-collecting services are concerned, and my only experience has been that they can often do little after you have already done your best, but could be worth trying.

Integrity in Different Lands

For the exporter, there are the additional problems, not found in the home market, of exchange control restrictions and sudden Government edicts in foreign countries which may prevent your customer from paying you at the due time, no matter how much he wants to. For this and other reasons, you ought to be extremely careful about dealing with people in under-developed countries.

In the following countries, most tradespeople are honest and usually pay: Canada, Australia, South Africa, New Zealand, Great Britain, Western European countries, Japan, U.S.A.

But even of the above, remember that the largest percentage of dishonest people are found in the big cities such as New York, Glasgow, and London.

On the other hand, in countries such as India, East and West Africa, the Middle East, and the Far East, as well as many other under-developed areas, you should work on the basis of not trusting anyone at all unless you know them very well. Goods can be shipped on a Cash With Order basis, or C.O.D. or care of the bank. Another method is to send goods against an Irrevocable Letter of Credit, and this is suitable for valuable consignments.

Any small business which has a large proportion of export turnover might well benefit from consulting the Export Credit Guarantee Department in the U.K., who are able to help and advise and have a great deal of experience.

Remember that one bad debt can lose the profit on twenty good sales.

Internal Systems

It may surprise you to know that I regard a desk diary as the most vital thing in your office. I have always used the diary system, and in almost any business it is essential.

I will set down a few uses that can be made of it. There are of course endless other uses which will occur to the reader for his particular business. A cheap diary is just as effective as a leather-bound affair.

(1) Either fill up and refer to the diary each morning yourself, or give the job to a trusted employee. I have tried second-rate assistants, and they either forget to enter items or omit looking for them each morning.

(2) Reliability is one of the foundations of a good business. In addition to the obvious use for appointments, your diary can be made to cover items in your programme which may lie months ahead. It works like an alarm clock to remind you of all needs at the right time. At the end of the diary, keep a few sheets of paper for items which are to be carried forward to the next year when you get your new diary.

(3) Extend the use of your diary to cover all sorts of items as they enter your mind. In this way, your memory is neither strained, nor excessively relied upon. Once you have put a thing in the diary, you can stop worrying about it until the reminder comes round.

Have a large enough space, preferably a whole page, for each day, and don't be afraid to fill in even trifling items, because, taken together, all such items result in efficiency, both in personal and in business affairs.

Here is a sample page:

FRIDAY, April 3rd

Wind office clock (repeated every Friday throughout the year).

Pay salaries (repeated every fourth Friday throughout the year).

Check deliveries for exhibition.

Is 'X's' order ready to send on Monday?

Post *Daily Telegraph* advertisement copy.

Have 'Y's' photographs been returned?

Oil electric fan (repeated every three months throughout the year).

Pay W. Wilson's account

Has 'Z' paid as promised for April 1st?

Check wear on front wheel tyres.

Phone Brown about contract.

Wedding anniversary tomorrow.

From this sample day, you can see how essentials are automatically brought to your notice. In time, customers and others will come to feel that they can depend upon you.

Dealing with Correspondence

In all but the smallest type of business, the partners or directors have to delegate work to other people.

I find that a large box beside my desk, near my hand is ideal. It is divided into compartments. Trays, drawers, or spikes, could equally serve. In my business, the mail which is opened is sorted into the appropriate box, and the compartments are cleared by our efficient staff who go off to their own sections and get on with their tasks.

Daily Letters and Problems

I find it best to keep these in one large pile. Numerous trays are a nuisance because you may need to go through them all anyway. Each day I check the pile methodically, keeping to the top and bringing up to the top all urgent items or those which are becoming urgent.

For orders awaiting confirmation, delivery notes, and orders which may have been held up pending a customer's payment, I use a bulldog clip which hangs on a nail. This occupies little room, and everyone knows where to find the item which is required.

Whatever systems you employ, make it your rule to keep them simple, nearby, and quick to use.

The Use of Banks

Most businesses have a bank account, and only a very tiny business could exist without one. The Post Office Giro System is like a bank, and works in the same way.

Banks have two main purposes, apart from lending money:

(1) To take care of your money.

(2) To enable you to pay by cheque, credit transfer, or standing order.

Ideally, all cheques, postal orders, and cash beyond immediate requirements should be banked daily. In practice, for a small business it may not be worth going to the bank for tiny sums every day. If you accumulate your cheques and postal orders, be sure to make them safe by having a rubber stamp. This reduces the risk of theft or eliminates the risk of embezzlement – indeed even a thief would find the cheques and postal orders useless. Our rule is to stamp every item as the envelopes are opened thus:

A/C ELLIOT RIGHT WAY BOOKS ONLY

For paying out money, the safest way is probably by cheque, because the returned used cheque provides proof of payment. An alternative method which can be used in some businesses is to pay by credit transfer. This is said to save bank charges, as you make out one cheque in order to pay a variety of different accounts. This method is probably only suitable where you have a large number of small suppliers. I doubt whether it is really worthwhile, as the alleged saving in bank charges may not outweigh the extra administrative cost and the earlier debiting of your account. In order to work the credit transfer system, you need to know the details of your supplier's bank account, branch, and account number.

If you pay by cheque, make sure that the cheques you send out are stamped or written across:

A/C PAYEE ONLY

or for 100% safety

A/C J. BLANK & CO. ONLY

We stamp all our cheques when we get a new cheque book so that this cannot be overlooked.

Bank charges can be a significant cost in the small business, and for this reason it may sometimes be advantageous to pay very small accounts by means of a postal order. Here you should fill in the name and town of the recipient, and also across the postal order:

A/C PAYEE ONLY, filling in the recipient's name.

Some of your customers may require receipts for their accounts. I hope that this can be discouraged because of the high cost of posting receipts. To save work, it is wise to have a receipt stamp made, which costs little.

4
TAX

We all complain of the tax inspector, and even poke fun at him. However, I believe that people are usually treated fairly.

The duty of the U.K. Inland Revenue is to get everything it is entitled to, but no more.

On the other hand, the right of the individual is to arrange his affairs in such a way that he pays the least tax he is lawfully allowed to. You therefore owe it to yourself, your family and your business to obtain all the allowances to which by law you are entitled.

A business of any size will employ an accountant or auditor. Your accountant is your guide, and he should be able to advise you of all the legal ways in which this or that item can be charged out of expenses, and not out of taxed income or capital.

Remember, however, that accountants are only human. Some of them perhaps prefer the 'easy life', and remember, it's not their money they are parting with. Accountants value the relationship that they have with the local Inland Revenue office, and some do not want to get a name for being 'troublesome'.

If you have cause to believe that your accountant is not pushing your interest as far as possible with the Revenue Authorities, then change your accountant.

Do not be under any misapprehension, however; the tax people can cause you considerable anxiety if they think that you are trying to swindle them. For instance, they can call for special accounts, perusal of receipts, and in extreme instances you may have to attend at the tax office for interview. All this can be extremely time-wasting, costly, and worrying. Sometimes the case can become most involved and difficult, and end you up in the Courts trying to argue things which are very hard to prove. The Authorities also have power to require you to produce documents, and can investigate your bank statements and can pry into your stock exchange deals.

Chargeable Expenses

Provided that you keep a note of all payments, then your accountant ought to be able to extract all business expenses in making up your profit and loss account. Obviously, you are not likely to overlook the cost of things that you buy, nor stationery, equipment, repairs, stocks, etc. Provided that you include these in your ledgers, and keep all the receipts, these items should prove no problem.

The difficulty arises with the more doubtful items. Here is a list of some common queries with some brief, basic guidance.

You are allowed to charge as a business expense special clothing required for the job, such as overalls, protective garments, etc., but you are not allowed to charge ordinary clothes and shoes which you would wear in daily life anyway.

You are allowed to charge subscriptions to trade associations and magazines.

You are allowed to charge books, especially technical books, which are essential for the business.

You are allowed to charge luncheon vouchers for your employees. If you run a canteen, you can charge the entire cost of this.

You are allowed to charge the cost of tools and machines used wholly and exclusively for business.

You are allowed to charge the cost of training schemes, conferences, etc., and bigger firms would be allowed to charge such items as the cost of the firm's dance or annual outing.

If you require a telephone in your home for the purposes of the business, you will be allowed to charge an appropriate proportion of the cost of it.

If you require a car or van for the purpose of your business, you would be allowed to charge the cost involved in running this, but if the car is owned by your *Company* then it may fall to be taxed as a 'benefit in kind' (in the U.K.) and could incur a tax liability on you personally, according to scales issued from time to time by the Inland Revenue. On this, you may need to seek the advice of your accountant. As far as entertaining is concerned, the cost of entertaining home customers is not allowed in the U.K. as a business expense before tax. However, one is allowed to charge as a business expense the cost of entertaining any overseas export customers.

As far as buildings are concerned, the cost of the buildings themselves (except for certain factories) are regarded as capital expenditure, and no allowance can be made for these. However, you can charge the cost of equipment and fittings, and you can also charge the cost of repairs and maintenance. However, a major job such as an extension to a building would have to be regarded as a capital cost.

There are special allowances available for investment in heavy machinery.

With items of this kind, and many others which may be doubtful, you must tell your accountant everything. Ask him the legal position, and cross-question him so as to be sure that you secure all you are entitled to.

Also, do not forget that the law enables you to reopen matters up to six years old in cases where errors have been made.

For instance, supposing you suddenly remembered that you had overlooked some essential piece of expenditure which had happened a few years before. In that case, provided that you could prove the spending, you would be able to reopen the matter with the tax authorities, and you should get a refund.

Your Wife or Husband

Many of the most successful small businesses are based on a husband and wife team. If both do an equal amount of work, then there will be little reason why each should not receive an equal share of the profits. I would strongly advise this in the case of more successful businesses, because in the U.K. a wife is now entitled to have her income assessed separately from that of her husband. Where the earnings of the business would be high enough to bring one person into the higher rates of income tax, this can be legitimately avoided by such a split. It would, however, only be allowed where both did an approximately equal amount of the work. However, where, say, the wife only did a small amount of the work, it would nevertheless be perfectly legal to pay her an appropriate amount of money for what is involved. For instance, if your wife is at home to receive telephone calls for you, or does a bit of typing for you in the evenings, or looks after the shop for one day of the week while you go to the market, there would be nothing wrong with paying a few pounds a week. Remember that if this amount is below the wife's earned income allowance, no basic rate tax would be payable on it at all unless she had other earnings. On this one, be guided by your accountant.

Personal Expenses

This can be *the* item of today, with high tax rates robbing the hard
worker. It is a sad fact that left-wing politicians seem to regard
businesses as an instrument for tax avoidance, rather than as a
means of contributing to the prosperity of the country. For this
reason, many things, like expense account lunches for entertaining home buyers, or medical insurance payments, have been
ruled out as legitimate business expenses. Today, vast numbers of
people, even many with very high salaries, get no expense allowances whatever. Naturally, the public are apt to feel sore if they
think that this or that business person gets an enormous expense
and/or car allowance. Many think that all allowances ought to be
stopped. Against such views, many businessmen feel extremely
sore on the grounds that they do not get enough.

Let me show you how complicated it all is. Where do business
expenses begin, and where do they end? Suppose I am a manufacturer of widgets working in Glasgow. I go to Bournemouth on
holiday, and I take my catalogue with me. While I am there, I call
on a big widget wholesaler who covers the whole of Southern
England. I golf two days with the proprietor. After two more
meetings at his premises, I obtain a contract with him to sell two
million widgets over the next five years. Let us suppose that this
shows me a profit of £20,000. I shall probably lose more than half
of that £20,000 in tax, because I am a high-rate tax payer. My
week's holiday cost me £200. Would you agree that I am entitled
to charge the expense of getting from Glasgow to Bournemouth
and back and indeed a good proportion of my hotel bill as well, if
not that of my wife's? On the other hand, could it not be equally
argued that we went on holiday for fun, and the other thing just
'happened'. On such matters, there is a very great deal of room
for doubt, and the individual must square his own conscience.

An honest man would probably charge £70 for the cost of the
motoring to and fro, and say three-fifths of his own hotel bill (but
not his wife's).

Take another case. A man who works like a slave is chairman
of a large company making £10 million for the shareholders per
year. His salary is £100,000 per year, but after tax he will get only
about half of this. He owns a large house in the country with a
three acre garden. From all over the world, export customers visit
him. He and his wife entertain these customers at their home.
Many may bring their wives and stay for a few days. Some of

these customers place orders worth hundreds of thousands of pounds, or millions.

The cost of running this house might well come to more than the chairman's salary after tax. He employs a gardener, a butler, and two house helps. Is he expected then to continue running his home and thereby ruining himself? No. The answer is he gets some thousands of pounds a year expense allowance. You might say, 'How unfair,' but stop and think. Could a man in that position expect his wife to spend her days gardening and scrubbing floors and cooking delicious meals, even if she was strong enough to do it all in so large a property? And she must be bright and gay to entertain those important customers. Again (you might say), let the chap go into a small house and entertain his guests in a hotel and get receipts for each item. If he took his wife and entertained lavishly, it might even come to more. So would the country be any better off?

In practice, however, overseas customers do not like to be entertained in hotels so well as in beautiful homes. Americans, in particular, just love the Elizabethan Manor. The big businessman couldn't possibly take them home to a small tenement. If we are quite honest, can we expect the chairman of a great concern to be worried as to whether he spends a little too much here or there, or whether by dismissing his gardener he can save £X a year by doing it at weekends himself?

He must remember that one of these customers may be in the market for £5 million worth of machinery. If the order can be won, the profit on the transaction might be three quarters of a million pounds. If the order is lost, it might go to Germany or America, to the detriment of the British balance of payments. The chairman probably works an average of fifteen hours a day and has ulcers.

I have mentioned all this to try and show what happens in practice. The Inland Revenue has the very difficult task of trying to do the right thing within the law. The results are not perfect but, with the law as it stands, are probably on the whole favourable to the Chancellor of the Exchequer, at least so far as honest people are concerned.

Inspectors of Taxes undoubtedly view things relatively. Thus if a Company chairman earning a salary of £100,000 for a Company making and being taxed on many millions claims £10,000 as travelling expenses and entertainment of overseas customers, it would probably be allowed.

If John Smith, the village grocer, earning £7,500 a year claimed £5,000 travelling expenses, the odds are that he would run into difficulty. On the other hand, a self-employed manufacturer's agent earning only £15,000 in commission might well claim £6,000 as travelling and subsistence expenses for his area of, say, the whole of Wales, and get it. He might, nevertheless, be required to produce receipts for the bulk of it.

Brown, a city solicitor, earning £10,000 a year, would probably experience no difficulty if he asked for £500 a year for travelling and subsistence.

This subject is beset with difficulties, because, even with receipts, swindling has been known. For example, the restaurant bill may not have been the foreign customer's at all, or the customers may be personal friends. Unknown to the accountant, that bill may have included 100 cigarettes for yourself. The bill for petrol may well have been for filling up your wife's car. And bills can be 'bought' from waiters!

Practical Advice for You

Be honest.

Do not try to cheat the Inland Revenue. They have long experience of comparing similar businesses, and many 'spy' methods of discovering swindlers.

Quite apart from the moral issue, experienced businessmen all have the same thing to say. 'It is not worth it.'

Let your motto be, 'Don't cheat the tax people but don't cheat yourself'.

Value Added Tax

In Great Britain and most European countries, Value Added Tax is the principal method of indirect taxation. It is administered in Great Britain by the Customs & Excise Authorities. If your business turnover exceeds the minimum which is laid down, then you are required by law to register with the Customs & Excise for Value Added Tax. After that, you have to fill in a form each quarter, and remit the amount of tax due. Businesses which deal in mainly zero rated goods may find that they are in fact entitled to a refund of Value Added Tax.

In order that your V.A.T. returns are accurate, it is essential to keep proper records of what are called 'inputs' and 'outputs'.

Inputs are the things that you buy for the purpose of your business. Usually this is mainly the goods which you are going to sell, but can also include such items as machinery, office equipment, etc. However, wages and salaries, postage stamps, rates, rents and insurances are not regarded as inputs.

Whenever you are charged for the goods that you buy, you will receive what is called a 'tax invoice'. This shows the amount of tax that you have been charged by your supplier. At the end of each quarter, you have got to make up a list of all these tax invoices charged during the quarter, so that you can arrive at a total of the amount of tax you have paid on your inputs.

Whenever you sell goods or services, you must charge the appropriate amount for Value Added Tax at the rate appropriate to the goods or service. In the United Kingdom, some goods are 'zero rated' which means that you do not include any element of tax in your retail price. Exports are also zero rated. For all other goods, you must include the amount of V.A.T. in the total price that you finally sell them for. You may choose to quote a price exclusive of V.A.T. and then add the V.A.T. on at the point of sale. Alternatively you may charge a complete price which includes the V.A.T.

At the end of the quarter, you furnish a return showing the total amount of goods that you have sold and the V.A.T. payable thereon. From this figure, you are entitled to deduct the V.A.T. that you have paid on the goods you have bought (your inputs). You send a cheque or do a credit transfer for the difference. If the total of V.A.T. on your inputs exceeds the V.A.T. on your outputs, then you receive a refund from the Customs & Excise.

There are special schemes for retailers which avoid the necessity of itemizing the amount of tax on each individual sale, where outputs are charged at different rates of V.A.T. Full details of these can be had from your local Customs & Excise office.

From what I have said above, you might think that it would be an easy matter to defraud both the Customs & Excise and the Inland Revenue by under-declaring your V.A.T. outputs. In fact, I believe that this would be extremely difficult to do, besides being morally wrong. The reason is that the Customs & Excise have experience in a very, very wide variety of different businesses, but they can tell the average relationship between V.A.T. inputs and outputs for different types of business. Any firm which varied much from the national average could immediately be spotted and pounced upon, and I must warn you that the Customs

Officers have very wide powers of searching and checking the premises of people who they believe have furnished suspect returns. As with income tax, honesty is the best motto.

The Records That Are Necessary

The first essential is a proper record of inputs. Books for entering these items can be obtained cheaply from stationers. You must keep a record of each invoice received, and write down in your V.A.T. book the total amount of V.A.T. charged thereon. You will need to keep a file of these invoices for some years afterwards, as Officers of Customs & Excise will visit your premises from time to time to check your returns. The amount of information which you need to put in the book should be sufficient to enable the Customs Officer to identify the particular invoice which is referred to.

You also need to keep proper records of the sales made, so that you can total the amount of invoices issued each quarter, and the amount of tax charged thereon. Alternatively, if yours is a cash business, you need to obtain an exact total of the amount of cash received each day, or week, so that you can make up a quarterly total. Fuller details of how to handle this for cash traders are to be found in the Special Schemes for Retailers which can be obtained free from your local Customs & Excise Office.

Remember that for V.A.T. purposes, the tax point is the date on which an invoice is *issued*, or the date of payment, whichever is *earlier*.

P.A.Y.E. and National Insurance Contributions

These are deductions which you must make from the wage or salary before you pay the money to your employee. It is rather complicated. All information can be obtained from your local Inland Revenue Office, and they will supply you with the necessary cards, tax tables, etc. There are various methods of working out P.A.Y.E. according to whether wages are paid monthly, four weekly, fortnightly, or weekly. The instructions which come with the cards must be followed exactly. Each month, payment is made to the Tax Authorities, of the Tax and National Insurance Contributions deducted from the wages. In April of each year, the completed cards are returned and new cards are received. Any bonus or overtime money or the like have to carry their share of tax.

Many employees do not like the people they work with to know how much they earn, and so normally it is best to keep these matters as private as possible. If you can pay at four weekly intervals it's a great time saver over weekly. We do!

5
LEGAL ASPECTS

Letter-headings

People judge you by your letter-heading, but it is perhaps not as important as some may suppose. Use good quality paper, and have an experienced printer do the layout. Embossed headings are costly, and few small firms have them. Two-colour printing can be more attractive than one but, unless yours is a business dealing a lot with the public or with people abroad, one colour, being cheaper, is enough. It need not be black, you can use a deep blue, green or red. Remember to put in the telephone number and STD code, and print it large enough so that one does not need a magnifying glass to read it.

On your letter-heading, you can also describe the nature of the business that you undertake.

Where you are trading under any name or names other than your own, for example, where you have bought an existing business, it must be registered under the Registration Of Business Names Act, within 14 days of commencing to trade. Before registering a name, you should also check that no-one else has Trade Mark rights in the name, by consulting the Trade Marks Registry.

Here are the legal requirements regarding letter-headings:

(*a*) The letter-heading must show the names of the partners or company directors. (Very large companies can claim an exemption from this.)

(*b*) Where you are trading as a company, the letter-heading must show the registered office of the company even if that is not the address from which the business is conducted. It must also show the place of registration, and the registration number of the company. This can be in small print, e.g.

"Registered in England No. 813524".

Contracts

Let the key word here be CARE. You must not only protect yourself against normal business risks, strikes, etc., but against the 'fly' individual who tries to find loopholes in your contract with which he can win money out of you in court, for some trifling reason. The main consideration must be the integrity of the firm you are dealing with. A contract can be full of loopholes if the other party to it is honest. On the other hand, the best contract in the world, drawn up by the ablest lawyer, is probably useless if you are dealing with a crook.

Contracts are usually required for long-term jobs, or where the conditions and specification are intricate and involved, or where records are required. Customs of trade come into the picture very much, and before you begin entering big contracts, you must be conversant with these customs and with the legal implications.

Trade Associations sometimes have specimen contracts or lists of clauses from which you can pick those which suit your business. Alternatively, a friendly competitor might let you use the wording he uses, or a customer might lend you a contract from another firm. In this instance, do realize that you must not copy the wording, owing to the law of copyright, unless you first obtain permission from the copyright holder. However, perusal of several different contracts in your own trade or profession should enable you to draw up, in your own words and sequence, whatever clauses you think you need. At that point, call in a good lawyer and get him to vet the clauses. It is better to be safe than sorry. Once you have got a good contract form, be cautious filling in the clauses. Never commit yourself unless you must, and you are sure that you can do all you undertake.

A Sample Contract

By way of illustration, I give below an example of the kind of contract that is used in the book publishing field, where long-term contracts with authors are normal. This is a contract with an author to publish his book on a royalty basis.

MEMORANDUM OF THE AGREEMENT made this ......
day of .... 19.... between ....
of ....
(hereinafter called 'The Author', which expression shall, where

the context admits, include the Author's executors, administrators and assigns), of the one part, and Elliot Right Way Books, Kingswood Building, Kingswood, Tadworth, Surrey, (hereinafter called 'The Publisher', which expression shall, where the context admits, include the Publisher's executors, administrators, and assigns, or successors in business as the case may be) of the other part.

Note that this binds the executors of the Author after he has died and would also bind any other firm who took over the publishing business.

WHEREAS the Author has written/is writing/is compiling/is editing/is translating a literary work at present entitled .... it is mutually agreed between the parties hereto as follows:

1. The Author assigns to the Publisher the copyright of the manuscript (at present in typescript form/still to be written) referred to above, and the right to publish it throughout the world.

2. The Publisher shall pay to the Author a royalty of ...... % on the retail price of each and every copy sold, except that no royalty shall be payable on copies remaindered at under half retail price.

A different clause 1 and 2 would apply in instances where the Author sold the book outright to the Publisher, as many do.

3. The rate of royalty stated above shall apply to the first ...... thousand copies sold, provided that this figure is reached within five years. After this figure has been reached, the royalty rate referred to in clause 2 above shall be increased to ...... %, while the other provisions of clause 2 above shall apply exactly as before. This clause shall not come into effect if the sales do not reach .... thousand copies within five years of the date of publication.

This type of clause allows the Author a higher royalty if sales are good. Obviously, if the sales are high, the Publisher can produce the books at a lower cost because of printing larger quantities, and in some circumstances it may be agreed that the Author should benefit from this. Conversely, of course, the inclusion of this clause might inhibit the Publisher from publishing a second or subsequent edition to the detriment of the Author. It would be possible for a Publisher who used this sort of clause to estimate how many the book was likely to sell, and then to offer the higher rate of Royalty on sales beyond this figure, knowing the probability that this 'carrot' would never come to be eaten.

4. On final acceptance of the manuscript it is agreed to pay a non-returnable advance against royalties of ....
(sum in words). When the advance is liquidated by the royalties, the ordinary royalty comes into effect as before per clause applying.

This clause might well apply to the best-selling type of Author, who felt he was on to a certainty and wanted to be sure of getting some money early.

5. The Author will submit to the Publisher a sample chapter and a synopsis of the work, for consideration, and he should await the Publisher's approval of this before writing the rest of the book. The Publisher reserves the right to cancel this Contract if, in his opinion, the book is not up to the standard of, and as good in literary and other merit, and marketability as, the sample or parts of the Author's work which have already been examined by the Publisher or his assistant.

By contrast, this clause might apply where an Author was inexperienced, and was in the process of writing a book which had been specially commissioned.

6. It is agreed that the book is to be approximately ...... words in length (including illustrations) and it must be written with the design of getting it into a total of ...... printed (not typescript) pages, leaving ...... pages for prelims/end page ads/index etc. (size crown octavo).

7. It is agreed that the Author will deliver the completed manuscript within ...... months of the date of this contract.

These two clauses also apply to books which are in the process of being written and signify proper agreement as to the length the book is to be and the date by which the manuscript is to be delivered.

8. Should extracts be taken, or overseas or other subsidiary rights sold from the book, including any right conferred by legislation in the future, any monies accruing therefrom shall be divided equally between the Author and the Publisher.

This clause applies to other uses that may be made of the copyright material, and entitles the Publisher to a share of the proceeds, which he is entitled to as he has taken the huge initial risk in publishing the book.

9. In the remote event of special printings of the book being sold in large quantities for 'give-away' or 'premium' offers, the Author shall receive 25% of the gross profit made on the deal by the Publisher.

This clause is entirely fair and saves the Publisher having to pay the full rate of royalty on large quantities of books sold for premium offers. The problem here can be that books sold as premium offers might well have no deemed retail price on them so the normal royalty rate could not be calculated as per contract anyway.

10. The Publisher shall render to the Author an account in December of each year (or within three months thereafter) after the date of publication, and the amount shown to be due in royalties, and in payments of the Author's share of the sales of subsidiary rights, to the end of November of that year, shall be paid to the Author at the time such an account is rendered. Should accounts and payments not be so rendered this contract shall be cancelled, and all rights shall revert to the Author without prejudice to monies due.

11. It is agreed that the Author through his/her accountants or solicitors shall have the right of access to the sales records of the Publisher to verify the figures should he/she so desire.

These two clauses protect the Author.

12. It is agreed that royalty figures shall not be adjusted on any title exchanges to oblige the trade, provided that such changes do not exceed 5% of any one title. (Authors should not lose by this clause, which brings considerable benefits in extra sales and goodwill.)

13. Should copies of the work be destroyed as a result of fire or flood, no royalties shall be paid on any of the copies destroyed.

These are normal clauses.

14. Should the book be allowed to go out of print for more than 18 months, all rights herein granted shall revert to the Author

after nine months' notice is given in writing to the Publisher, without prejudice to any monies due.

This protects the Author in the event of the book going out of print. Clearly most books have a limited life, and eventually the decision has to come that it is not worth printing any more. This decision has to be taken by the Publisher. If the Author disagrees with this decision, then the Author can have the copyright of the book back, and can attempt to sell the book to another Publisher.

15. The Author agrees to make any necessary alterations at the manuscript stage if possible, owing to the high cost of proof corrections. If the cost of corrections to the proofs exceeds $7\frac{1}{2}\%$ of the total cost of composition, the excess is to be deducted from the Author's royalties.

This is important owing to the very high cost of making corrections, which could otherwise wreck the Publisher's costing system.

16. It is understood that any revision shall be carried out promptly by the Author should this be required. In the event of the Author's death or any disagreement, the Publisher shall retain the right to employ any party qualified to do such revision; the cost of same, if any, being deducted from royalties.

This clause is especially important for books which may go out of date and protects the Publisher if he finds that he has an un-co-operative Author of a best-seller.

17. Authors are informed that the Inland Revenue Tax Authorities have the power to make Publishers disclose royalties paid to Authors, and to disclose the Author's name and address.

This clause may perhaps not be strictly necessary, but is designed to save Authors trouble that could be caused if they overlooked the requirement to disclose the royalties paid to them on their Annual Income Tax Return form.

18. It is understood that the Publisher shall be allowed to attend to minor editing and revision of the book.

19. Publication of the book shall be arranged as soon as possible, making allowance for any bottlenecks of production, and for fitting into the Publisher's programme.

20. The Publisher is to have entire control of the publication and

the paper, printing, binding, jackets/cover, etc., and will do all he can to promote sales.

21. The Publisher may publish a second, or subsequent editions, and the question of selling price must be left to his discretion.

22. It is understood that all corrections to proofs shall be undertaken promptly by the Author.

23. The present title is not necessarily final; for instance, various legal difficulties could prevent its use. It is agreed that the choice of title will finally be left to the Publisher, but that any alternative suggestions will receive consideration.

24. It is understood that no other book will be written by the Author which could conflict with the sale of this one.

All these clauses are designed to protect the Publisher against problems of the kinds which have arisen in the past.

25. The Author warrants the Publisher that the said work is in no way a violation of any existing copyright and that it contains nothing obscene, objectionable, indecent or libellous, nor any information prohibited under the Official Secrets Acts, and will indemnify the Publisher for any loss, injury or damage, including any legal costs or expenses properly incurred by the Publisher, in consequence of any breach of this warranty.

This clause is designed to frighten off Authors who are going to copy other people's work, and to protect the Publisher to some degree against the cost of litigation for libel, etc. Needless to say, any question of libel is extremely serious for the Publisher, as he would probably have to withdraw the book from sale or at least stand the cost of issuing erratum slips, so great care is always taken with this subject.

26. The Author warrants the Publisher that he is free to write for the Publisher and is not tied under Contract or in any way to any other publisher.

This clause is included because many Publishers 'tie' the Author to offer them, say, the next three books that they write. This applies especially to fiction. After a Publisher may have spent many thousands of pounds in promoting and advertising an Author's first book, in the hope of getting the pay-off with subsequent books, this can be seen not to be entirely unreasonable. However, another Publisher could be in difficulty if an Author

*broke this undertaking with his first Publisher, which is the
reason for this clause.*

27. The Publisher agrees to distribute review copies of the book,
and to give six copies to the Author on publication. Further
copies can be supplied to the Author at a discount of one third off
the retail price.

28. The Publisher retains the right, in the event of extreme circumstances such as war, or Government action or interference
which would make completion impracticable, to amend or even
to cancel this Contract.

*This is trying to foresee the totally unforeseeable, but the sort
of eventuality that the Publisher would have in mind, apart from
the case of war, would be such a thing as the imposition of import
controls which made it impossible for him to get paper to print
the book on. Another possibility would be the passing of new
legislation which totally forbade the activity that the book sought
to instruct.*

29. The Author shall keep a carbon copy of the manuscript as a
protection against loss. It is agreed that the Publisher shall not
insure manuscripts, photographs or drawings, etc., placed in his
possession and shall not be liable for loss thereof.

30. The Publisher hopes that the Author will give him first refusal of any other manuscript written by him in the future.

*As stated above, a much stronger clause than this is very com-
mon, in which the Author is required to give the Publisher first
refusal of the next two or three books that he writes, for publication on the same terms and conditions.*

31. It is understood that the book is to be written under the
Author's own name. Please give, in block capitals, own surname
and Christian names in full ....
.... also, if agreeable, please give date of birth
.... This information is required by the British
Museum Copyright Department for full identification of
Authors.

*This is not really part of the Contract, but gives the Publisher
access to the information necessary for proper establishment of
the copyright in the book.*

32. The rights and obligations under this Agreement shall be

binding upon the Author and Publisher respectively and shall belong to and be binding upon their personal representatives, assigns and successors in business where applicable.

AS WITNESS the hands of the parties this .... day of .... 19....

Signature ....

Signature
of witness ....
(Not a relation)

Address
of witness ....

....

Occupation of witness ....

Normally in such a contract as this, two copies of the Contract would be made, one would be signed by the Publisher and given to the Author, the other would be signed by the Author and given to the Publisher. A witness to the signature on both sides is necessary, in order to make the document legally binding.

Quotations

Questions of costing and pricing are discussed fully in Chapter 7. From the legal point of view, you are well advised to be extremely cautious, and to include any necessary disclaimers. For instance, if you are a garage, say,

'Cars driven at owners' risk.'

If a laundry,

'While every care is taken of customers' orders, no responsibility can be accepted for damage, shrinking or fading.'

It might also be advisable to post such disclaimers as large notices on your premises.

Be guided in such matters by the custom of your trade. I have not given exact wordings to use, but I merely mention the matter so that it will not be forgotten, as omission could be very costly.

As an example of the type of thing that can be required, I give below the standard conditions of sale of a printing company.

STANDARD CONDITIONS

1. COST VARIATION. – Quotations are based on the current costs of production and are subject to amendment by the printer on or at any time after acceptance to meet any rise or fall in such costs.
2. VALUE ADDED TAX. – The printer shall be entitled to charge the amount of any V.A.T. payable whether or not included on the quotation or invoice.
3. PRELIMINARY WORK. – Work produced, whether experimentally or otherwise, at customer's request will be charged for.
4. PROOFS. – Author's corrections on and after first proof, including alterations in style, will be charged extra. Proofs of all work may be submitted for customer's approval, and no responsibility will be accepted for any errors in proofs passed by him.
5. DELIVERY AND PAYMENT. – Delivery of goods shall be accepted and payment shall become due upon notification that they are ready for delivery.
6. EXPEDITED DELIVERY. – Should expedited delivery be agreed and necessitate overtime or other additional cost, an additional charge may be made.
7. VARIATIONS IN QUANTITY. – Every endeavour will be made to deliver the correct quantity ordered, but quotations are conditional upon a margin of 5% (in colour work 10%) being allowed for overs or shortage, the same to be charged for or deducted.
8. CLAIMS. – Claims arising from damage, delay, or partial loss of goods in transit must be made in writing to the printer and the carrier so as to reach them within 3 days of delivery and claims for non-delivery within 28 days of despatch of the goods. All other claims must be made to the printer within 10 days of delivery.
9. LIABILITY. – The printer shall not be liable for indirect or consequential loss or for any loss to the customer arising from third party claims occasioned by errors in carrying out the work or by delay in delivery.
10. STANDING MATTER. – Type may be distributed and lithographic, photogravure, or other work effaced immediately after the order is executed, unless written arrangements are

made to the contrary. In the latter event, rent may be charged.

11. CUSTOMER'S PROPERTY AND PROPERTY SUPPLIED. –

(*a*) Customer's property and all property supplied to the printer by or on behalf of the customer will be held at customer's risk.

(*b*) Every care will be taken to secure the best results where materials or equipment are supplied by customers, but responsibility will not be accepted for imperfect work caused by defects in or unsuitability of such materials or equipment.

(*c*) Where the customer supplies materials, adequate quantities shall be supplied to cover spoilage.

12. GENERAL LIEN. – The printer shall in respect of all unpaid debts due from the customer have a general lien on all goods and property in his hands and shall be entitled on the expiration of 14 days' notice to dispose of such goods or property as he thinks fit and to apply the proceeds towards such debts.

13. ILLEGAL MATTER.

(*a*) The printer shall not be required to print any matter which in his opinion is or may be of an illegal or libellous nature.

(*b*) The printer shall be indemnified by the customer in respect of any claims, costs and expenses arising out of any illegal or libellous matter printed for the customer or any infringement of copyright, patent or design.

14. PERIODICAL PUBLICATIONS. – A contract for the printing of periodical publications may not be terminated by either party unless written notice is given as follows:

Nature of Publication	Length of Notice
Weekly	One Month
Fortnightly	Two Months
Monthly	Three Months
Quarterly	Six Months

Nevertheless, the printer may terminate any such contract forthwith should any sum due thereunder remain unpaid.

15. FORCE MAJEURE. – Every effort will be made to carry out the contract but its due performance is subject to cancellation by the printer or to such variation as he may find necessary as a result of inability to secure labour, materials or supplies or as a result of any Act of God, War, Strike, Lockout or other

labour dispute, Fire, Flood, Drought, Legislation or other cause (whether of the foregoing class or not) beyond the printer's control.

16. Every care is taken in the preparation of drawings and metal sheets. Before printing, metal sheets should be carefully checked to make sure that they comply with your requirements. In the event of an error being made, our liability shall be limited to the replacement or correction of the goods supplied.

You will see from clauses 1 and 15 that virtually every possible eventuality is taken care of, and in fact you could possibly argue that the quotation on the other side of the sheet of paper is scarcely more than an indication of the likely price. That would be the legal position, but from long experience we have in fact found the printers do always stick to their prices in an honourable manner.

Simple Sale Notice or Enquiry Form

There is much to be said for the Simple Sale Note or Confirmation Note, where some time is needed for delivery. This gives the customer a record for his files, and it may save disagreement as to what price was arranged, etc. The Enquiry Note can embody any special trade customs or conditions.

6
PERSONNEL

One of the new businessman's principal worries is obtaining good staff. Potential employees tend to prefer established firms, and these firms may obtain all the best staff in the area. Nevertheless the problem can usually be solved, if you go about it wisely.

There are all sorts of go-ahead people who want the opportunity that they feel the new firm may provide. Younger workers may consider the chances of quick promotion are greater with the new business, so do not despair.

There is also the type of person who prefers to work in a small firm – who would like to be a big fish in a small pool, rather than a tiny fish in the ocean. A lot of our fellow countrymen despise the thought of being one tiny cog in the wheel of some gigantic enterprise, and they prefer the opportunity to display their initiative and enthusiasm.

A good staff gives you the essential foundation for success. Do not become a haven for local duds. With them, you are as good as sunk, but with an outstanding staff you may succeed rapidly. So, cast wide your net, but in your natural anxiety to engage someone do not rush at it. Inferior staff are easier to get than to get rid of, and none of us likes sacking people. Often, second-raters never give you a cast-iron excuse for paying them off. They usually seem to do their best, but that may not be enough for the small struggling firm. You dare not have inefficient people at this stage.

Advertising

So important is the staffing problem that you should not be afraid to spend money on it.

Use every legitimate and decent method you can think of. In some cases, the Department of Employment will be your source, but in many instances the local paper, trade paper, or local comprehensive school are the most likely places to try. Also use other means, postcards in all the shop windows for miles around, or word of mouth may bring the right person. Your postman, milk-

man, local clergyman or anyone may know just the person you
seek.

The Law

Firstly, it is illegal to approach other firms' employees while they
are on the job. Secondly, try not to poach your local competitors' employees anyway. If such people reply to your advertisements, that is perhaps another matter. Even so, it is
generally unwise to accept staff from neighbouring competitors
as this is apt to cause ill-feeling, and may be reciprocated at a
later date when labour is extremely short, and you are desperate
for staff yourself.

Interviewing

Large firms may use intelligence tests, aptitude tests, and subject
applicants to a highly sophisticated battery of assessment pro-
grammes. Nevertheless, all of them probably come down in the
end to the good, old-fashioned method of interviewing, before
making their final decision.

Interviewing applicants is an art which cannot be taught in a
book like this one. It takes years of experience, and it also takes a
good deal of 'flair' or 'hunch' to pick out the right person.

Try to put an applicant at ease, by discussing such subjects as
holidays, pastimes, or sport.

See whether you can tell if you are going to get on well together,
and have a general chat covering previous experience, school life,
or work.

Where the work you are offering is of a semi-skilled kind, it is a
good idea to give a trial of work. For instance, if you are engaging
an invoice clerk, show how your invoices are done, and then give
a few invoices to do as samples.

Remember that many applicants are in a state of nerves, so if
you can let them do their sample work in another room, it gives a
better result. A typist or secretary can be tested with a few letters
dictated, then typed back, and so on.

Don't forget, however, that the world is full of people who are
excellent at tests, but useless on the job; the sort of people who
can concentrate quite all right for ten minutes or so, but who will
sit and chatter in the office or factory for hours on end disturbing
everybody else if you take them on.

A word of warning about school leavers. Gone are the days, I am afraid, when you could assume that a school leaver would be able to read and write properly. There is no question that the general standard of education of school-leavers is declining rapidly, particularly in our large cities. A very high proportion of them, unfortunately, seem unable to string two words together, to write a coherent letter, or even to add up simple lists of figures.

Nowadays I never take on a school leaver without asking him or her to take a simple arithmetic test, and to write a hand-written letter of application, explaining why he or she wants this particular job. Of course, this may not matter so much in business where there is little reading or writing involved, but the apparent inability of many school leavers to add or multiply could be very important in a shop.

The Wage or Salary

Ask the applicant how much he wants. Usually it is not wise to offer less, otherwise the applicant may not be happy. Good staff are usually well worth what they ask. Bad staff can cost you more than you save on a lower salary.

However, the exception would be where there is a pretty general 'going rate for the job' in the locality. Where this is the case, you might get the 'try on' where the prospective employee hopes that you, the new businessman, will pay way over the odds. Where this is the case, it should be obvious as there ought to be a number of other applicants willing to work for less.

References

The worst people that I have had anything to do with have always had excellent references.

The reference that is worth most is the one that you get direct, probably on the 'phone, from a previous employer whom you know. Another good one would be a reference written on the letter-heading of a reputable firm, provided it is not forged. In any event, if you do not feel that you are a confident judge of character, it is best to take up the reference by telephone, with one of the partners, or in the case of a limited company, the Company Secretary or a Director.

Understand the differences between a reference and a testimonial. A testimonial is a letter which is given to an employee on leaving, and might run something like this:

'To Whom it may Concern.

Miss XXXX has been employed by us for six months. During that time she has gained valuable experience of accounting procedures including comptometer operating. We have found her cheerful and good natured at all times, and we wish her the best in her future career.'

Frankly, this kind of thing does not mean much, and it is the sort of testimonial you *could* give to somebody you have had to sack for incompetence. I would be extremely suspicious of anybody who came along with one like that. On the other hand, a 'reference' is when the prospective employee gives you the name and address of his or her previous employer for you to contact them. Best to do this by 'phone if you want the real truth.

The reference of 'time' is good, if true. Usually the employee who has served ten years with one firm is worthy.

I personally think that by far the best plan is to get young staff and train them. Among the advantages are that you are not saddled in your old age with a lot of old people to pension off or try to retain out of decency. Also, most people are very hidebound in their attitudes, and few over 35 are capable of much change. If you take an employee of fifty, do it with your eyes open. Most likely the person will be so set in his methods that you will never get him round to your way. This can be irritating.

On the other hand, the youngster under 21 is usually flexible and teachable. You can show him quick ways and he will grasp them. Often, too, younger people have a more up-to-date idea of the value of money.

The Safety Valve

Whatever happens, engaging staff is a hit or miss thing. You will always make mistakes, and it is therefore wise to have a trial period.

Arrange that you will take the new employee for a week, two weeks, or a month's trial, whichever you prefer. At the end of that time, both sides are free to say whether or not they wish to continue. This gives both a good 'let out' should judgement have proved faulty.

Points to Watch

Before taking someone on, ask yourself (or the applicants) the following questions.

1. Does he look happy?
2. Does he look honest?
3. Does he appear suited/is he qualified for this particular job?
4. Does he seem intelligent?
5. Does he appear to like you?
6. Why did he leave his previous job?

Beware of the following

1. The person who stresses references.
2. The person who talks too much.
3. The person who promises you the moon.
4. Anyone who does not appear happy by nature.
5. Anyone who stresses their own honesty – these are usually the crooks.

Contract of Employment

In the United Kingdom, anybody who is taken on as a permanent employee is entitled to receive a contract of employment, under The Contract of Employment Act, 1963, and subsequent legislation.

Briefly, this contract must give the particulars of the terms and conditions of employment, as follows:

Rate of pay, dates on which pay is paid, and job title.
Normal hours of work and entitlement to lunch-hour and other breaks.
Holiday entitlement.
Procedure for making up pay during illness, if any.
Whether there is a pension scheme.
Length of notice of termination to which the employee is entitled.
(There is a legal minimum.)
Procedure for taking up grievances and disciplinary complaints.
Disciplinary rules.

Some employees may want complicated service contracts, which might be very difficult and expensive to break. I would advise strongly against these, initially at any rate. Give your employees the ordinary length of termination of notice as required by the law, but no more.

At a later date, a loyal employee might feel he deserves a better service contract, but it should be considered later, rather than earlier.

An example of a typical contract of employment is given in the Appendix, page 119.

Personnel Management

Dealing with staff may be more difficult than running the business. Large concerns usually employ personnel managers who receive large salaries. The position of personnel manager calls for the skill of an ambassador; indeed, that in a way is what he is, an ambassador on behalf of the company to its staff.

Consider the costs. What does it cost to train a skilled man? Perhaps as little as £500, but probably nearer £5,000, or even more. What folly to risk losing such a valuable asset to a competitor, for lack of a good relationship.

If multi-million pound concerns consider it vital to have a personnel manager and department, how much more important it is that you, the new entrant to business, should know a good deal about this matter.

Trade Unions

As the reader may know, the majority of large firms in the manufacturing industry, and some elsewhere, are trade union houses, whereas probably most small businesses are non-union. This book is mainly for the latter. It is also probably true that the majority of office staff, the so-called white collar workers, are non-union, or not much interested in unions especially if they work for small firms.

This book is not intended to be a political one, but I feel I should point out what I believe to be the main effect of Trade Union activity, because it has an effect on business. The British Trade Union leader tends to be very interested in getting as much money as possible and in keeping members at work. He is also interested in the welfare side, and in increasing benefits and holidays, etc., where possible. This has led to such a mass of restrictive practices, and overmanning, that the economy is endangered, and the money needed to pay these high wages simply is not forth-coming from the business. This tends to bring all workers down to a lower level, and I cannot believe it is a sound, long-term policy either for the country, the firms, or for the employees, except for the slackers. It is an economic fact that if a firm does not make big profits, it cannot pay big wages.

By contrast, the American or European Trade Union boss goes all out to get as much money for his members as he can, and to this end he encourages hard work and high productivity so that the companies make big profits from which high wages can be extracted.

For these reasons, I believe it is to the best advantage of the British business to avoid being a Union House which is perhaps best done by staying fairly small, by rewarding good workers extremely well, and by avoiding employing people who seem to be communist types bent on destroying society. For another thing, your staff save the Union subscription, so they get more money in their pockets even if you only pay Union rates. Unions don't run on air.

Attitude Towards Employees

One of the great, yet sad, things about Britain is that in the past there has been an immense difference in brain power, knowledge, and social background between what might be called the leaders and the general body of workers. I am sure that in few countries has this difference been so great, and it often leads to mis-understandings.

It is now changing, and this is welcome, owing to the greater opportunities for further education, greater social mobility, more employment opportunities, and the impact of television which educates the easy way while entertaining. TV might be called the poor man's university.

The master and servant relationship has been altered for the better by these things. It would be going too far to say that there are no longer masters, or servants! But the two, once poles apart, have moved closer. The master is not now dealing with sheer ignorance in the way that he used to – I mean ignorance in general, for our old-time worker was the world's best at his *job*. He is now dealing with a better educated person. Here lies opportunity, but also danger.

The employer aiming to run his business as a 'happy ship', a difficult thing to do, knows the wisdom of frequent talks with his staff and explanations of policy. Staff are human beings, and it is a help to them if they know some of the reasons why things are done, or why they are done a particular way.

Broadly speaking the more they know about their job, and about the firm's policy, the more interest they will show in their work. Do not be afraid to tell them if trade is unprofitable, or if it is good. Do not fear to ask for extra effort when things are in a rush. The result will show on whom you can depend for loyalty and good work. Do not hesitate to reward, if you can, your best staff, either with a rise, a bonus, or a share of profits, or some combination of these. It is from your best staff that you will find your leaders when your business expands.

Nor is money everything. Give praise where due. Few things are more delightful to staff than a feeling that they have been noticed or that their work is appreciated.

If you sometimes bring a few sweets or flowers for the office, it helps everyone. Birthdays can also be remembered for young staff up to 18.

Uninteresting Jobs

In most businesses there exist uninteresting jobs, or dirty or dull jobs. Of old, the less well-educated staff were given these soul-destroying jobs and put in the boring departments for life. Fifty years ago, the employer's difficulty was to find enough educated and intelligent people to do the interesting work.

Today the position is reversed. With more, if not better education, and higher expectations, the problem is to find people who will tackle the boring work. The symptom of this problem is the high wage which the poorer job carries, and the relative erosion of salaries received by the skilled or managerial types.

Make no mistake, these dull jobs are such a problem that in most businesses they require much consideration if staff are to be contented.

Making it Fun

In some types of work background music may prove a great anti-dote to boredom.

Where possible, allow the dull jobs to accumulate, and instead of, say, having one man or woman doing them all the time, have one or two days a month when the entire staff get together to do all the dull work. If people can laugh and chat while doing repetitive work, time goes faster.

Another plan is to employ part-time staff for the dull tasks. The young mother or the shift-worker who can only spare two to four hours a day is less likely to become unhappy, especially if the cash is needed.

One way of getting repetitive work done well is to pay a little extra or a bonus, or to introduce piecework rates. The latter can have a startling effect on efficiency.

Nearly all of us think that the other person's job is interesting, and our own one is dull. Well, even the exciting jobs get boring in time. Can you imagine anything duller than being a surgeon removing your thousandth appendix?

At first the newspaper sub-editor finds his work thrilling, but after a year it becomes routine.

In every department of your business, you can bring in modern methods to ease boredom. Visit business efficiency exhibitions and read business magazines to get new ideas. Never tire of asking your staff, especially department heads, for ideas of new and improved methods.

Adding machines, calculators and the like come to mind. These modern devices need not be feared, if used intelligently. Personnel using such mechanical aids need instruction, but they must be told to use common-sense as well.

To explain. When they use the calculator to find out how much 82 at 4p comes to and the answer comes up as £328, they must realize that they have made a mistake with the decimal point. By a rough mental double-check, 82 times 4p is obviously £3·20 something, so something over £300 cannot be right.

Similarly with an adding machine, that long column of figures on the roll could not possibly be £512, for at a glance you can see that it is well over £2,000. You can add the figures up and then down on the machine, as a check, but the rough check with the eyes should be used as well, in order to prevent that ghastly blunder involving a large error. The one type of error that never should be made.

Frequently routine work can be almost cut out by using rubber stamps or printed or duplicated forms. There are few things more pleasing to the boss than the staff who finds ways of reducing repetitive work. Remember that few jobs are dull if they only take a short time. It is the work that goes on day after day that kills enthusiasm. Please train your staff to change their work every two or three hours if possible. Even a change from one dull task to another can be cheering.

Holidays and Outings

In most business, three weeks' paid holiday is probably the rule. Some firms may give more after long service.

Most of us are work slaves. The boss may slave harder than his staff, but he has one thing they normally do not. He can take a day off. He can even take two days off. Although he works hard, he is free to choose. He may never take his extra two days, but he knows that if his brother asks him to Aberdeen for the long weekend he can go. The employee cannot, at least not without asking, and many do not care to ask. So why not consider if you could do this for your staff?

Give them one extra day off, per year, after the first year, for five years, so that when they have been with you for six years, they get a whole extra week. A week is not long, and if possible allow them to pick their own time for it and divide it up into individual days if need be, so long as it does not conflict too greatly with the running of the business.

These few extra days are what people want. You may have to stipulate that they are not joined to the yearly holiday entitlement, but apart from that try to be flexible.

Your staff will thank you for this consideration, especially the young, single ones. What they gain in health will probably more than compensate you financially because they may be less often ill.

If you feel that your business cannot afford this amount of holiday, consider a similar arrangement for extra days without pay.

I attach great importance to flexibility of working hours. A number of very big firms have recently come up with an idea of completely flexible working, in which the employees can come into work more or less when they like so long as they put in the requisite number of hours per week. This may not be possible for every employer, but there should be no reason why a person can't have half a day off one week, and make up for it by working the extra hours during the next.

Taking work home to make it up is not in my experience satisfactory. Unless staff are quite exceptionally honest, they are apt to claim for more hours work at home than they actually did. Even if they are honest about this, other staff could be jealous and it can lead to muddles.

The few minutes tea or coffee break at mid-morning and mid-afternoon are so common in offices that they hardly call for comment. Common-sense and control is required here as in everything. With heavy manual work, a full fifteen minutes or even thirty minutes break may be beneficial. This especially applies where hours are long.

But for businesses which work only 9 to 5 and a five day week, the employer should watch that he is not taken advantage of. With such work, a few minutes is all that is required.

Staff Training

In recent years, this has become an enormous industry in the U.K. Since the Industrial Training Act, 1964, employers have been able to claim grants towards the cost of certain kinds of training, and these grants have usually been easiest to claim where the training was of a kind which is particularly unsuitable for employees of the small business. For example, formal conferences in the 'poshest' hotels, sophisticated training plans, and people being sent away for weeks to learn methods which may be totally unsuitable for your business.

All in all, this type of 'official' training has very little relevance to the smaller business and is but another cause of inflation and heavy taxes.

Training staff is very time-consuming. On the whole, you are best to have one really intelligent employee, and train him or her. Then that person can be appointed to train the others and supervise. Training is really a part of management. New staff need watching, and your manager or trainer should watch them because you usually will not have the time.

The main secret of staff training is to go into detail. Not only show the person how to do the job, make sure they really understand how to do it, and that they understand the reason behind it. This helps the employee to see why it is so important.

Training goes on for years. You must always try to increase the usefulness of your staff because it will help you and because it gives them a chance to learn more and thus become more useful people. If they leave you to work somewhere else, they will be properly trained.

Staff will always make errors. New staff make more errors than older ones. Their work therefore needs a lot of supervision. Give everyone a chance. Point out mistakes courteously. Most people are trainable, but here and there you come across someone who either cannot improve because of lack of brain, or because of lack of interest. If you have no work for the less intelligent, you will have to get rid of them; those who are not interested should be paid off. They create a bad atmosphere as well as being useless to you.

So far as you can, aim to promote everybody up to work which will use all their skill and ability. When you do get that rarity – a good, intelligent, loyal employee – try to raise his salary and give promotion before it is asked for. Hold your best staff is a good motto.

Many people only rise to their full height when given opportunity. Trustworthy people deserve more freedom and more responsibility. When success expands your business, the key people will come from your present young staff. That young clerk you have got, let him try his hand at costing or looking after insurance. Yes, you will need to keep a check until you know he is safe. The keen warehouse worker, why not in quiet times send him out to see some customers for himself, or to try his hand at office work. Your typist; do you need to dictate all those simple letters? Have you tried letting her do them. You can catch the mistakes, if any, when you sign them. When you can trust her, she can sign all unimportant letters on your behalf.

If you fail to make full use of your staff, you only tire yourself out with detail and strain. How can you get the ideas and make the plans on which success depends if you are exhausted? Let every single member of the staff rise to his ceiling.

Planning the Work

If you have a number of staff, give a lot of thought to this. You will find that some of them are adept at, say, routine work, others at the more involved jobs. The wise employer puts everyone to the work he is happy at, and tries to fit the square pegs into the square holes. If you have only one employee or secretary, the same principle applies. Allocate to him or her the items that he or she can do as well as, nearly as well as, or better than you.

See that your staff have their work arranged first thing in the morning. Endless hours are lost and wasted by people hanging around and waiting for their tasks to be given to them. If this is not possible, then you must plan skilfully and arrange that each member of the organization has work in hand on which they can fall back in the event of your being unable to sort out their job until later in the day.

'Situations, Rows and Scenes'

These can be difficult. Many businesses are damaged by staff problems – jealousy, quarrelling, talking, dodging work, etc., and even stand-up fights.

You must not allow rows. Cultivate and insist upon courtesy between all staff, and if you hear hot words, go out and calm the culprits. You can tell them life is too short for that sort of thing.

Arguments and fights usually build up over a long period, and you should be able to spot them coming. Where two people who sit together do not get on well, it may be possible to separate them and put them in different rooms. Or at least quite a long way apart. If you have a really major row, call in both protagonists separately and hear both sides of the story. Then try and calm it down.

If one particular employee keeps getting into rows with the others, you may come to the conclusion that he is a trouble-maker. Get rid of these. You cannot afford to keep them.

On the other hand, there are people who have sickness at home, domestic or marriage problems, or onerous home duties. This is the kind of reason why perfectly good employees can fly off the handle occasionally. In these instances, sympathy is more often what is required, and occasionally as employer you may be able to help your employees to overcome their difficulties. Remember that nearly everybody has problems of one kind and another. Many homes are dreary, and filled with dreary people. That is why it is vital to cultivate a cheerful office, where everybody is as happy and as gay as possible. One of the secrets of getting through jobs is to like them and to enjoy the working conditions and to like the workmates.

Discharging Staff

You will be a lucky employer if the need for this never arises. Getting rid of duds, the dishonest, and trouble-makers will probably be the most frequent reason. Remember this. Everybody wants to save face. Nobody likes to be paid off for incompetence or laziness.

The person who does not work well for you may turn out wonderfully for some other employer. People react to each other differently. Your employee may have some unconscious dislike of you, which undermines his happiness and usefulness. There may be no serious fault on either side other than this incompatibility.

The Law entitles any employee with 26 weeks or more of continuous service to ask for a written statement of the reasons for dismissal. This means that you need to have a proper procedure for dismissals, and a complete record kept of misconduct, laziness, time-wasting, poor workmanship, troublemaking or whatever the problem may be. Vague descriptions are not likely to be enough because there is a type of person who complains to an Industrial Tribunal that the dismissal was 'unfair', and such applications, if successful, can cost you a great deal of money in compensation.

For these reasons, it is far wiser to use diplomacy. Sometimes it is possible to choose a moment for a person to go without actually having a stand-up row and sacking him. It is on the whole better if he thinks he is leaving of his own volition.

For instance, perhaps a person will ask for a salary increase which you can say that you cannot afford, and suggest that he might be able to do better elsewhere, where his talents would be better suited. Or perhaps trade will be quiet for a few days, and you can explain that things are looking sticky and the person cannot look forward to very good prospects with your firm.

These laws for employment protection are supposed to benefit workers, but I would argue that their real effect is exactly the opposite. Because it is so difficult to dismiss an employee, it means that all businessmen have to be far more selective than formerly about the people they take on. Gone are the days when you could easily 'give the young fellow a chance' and get rid of him if he didn't make the grade. Today, every decision about taking on new staff must be considered with the greatest care with the aim of excluding anybody who is not thought certain to be of the right quality.

Immediate Dismissal

Perhaps for theft, gross misconduct or insubordination, a person has to be 'sacked on the spot'. Fortunately this happens rarely.

Theft will perhaps be the most common reason in a small business. Here proof is difficult and you must be absolutely certain that you can prove it, as the person may protest innocence and demand a written statement of the reasons for dismissal and have you up before an Industrial Tribunal.

Temptation

If you put temptation in the way of people who haven't got much money, are you not maybe as much to blame as they? Where there is risk of loss by theft, see that you have checking systems. Wisdom suggests that you have an arrangement whereby staff can buy any of your goods that they want at a discount.

Where, however, you do get someone stealing, you are faced with a choice of either dismissing them or giving them another chance.

The decision depends on several things. Mainly, I think, the age and home background of the thief. If they are under 21 and especially from a poor home, a severe talking to should be worth trying. If you can convince them of the evil and folly of stealing, there should be a chance of cure. With the older types, I am afraid that wisdom indicates they must go. Older thieves have doubtless withstood many lectures.

Punishment

If guilt is proved or admitted, instant dismissal without pay is a severe punishment, make no mistake. The loss of wages is the least; the fact that the employee gets no reference is the main hardship, and one which can have a long-term effect. He also has to find a job, often very difficult with a bad record or lack of a recent reference.

Remember that no sins are so black that they do not qualify for forgiveness in the end. Not all employers are themselves perfect. Your worker may know a thing or two about you. He may after all have been stealing from you because he thought you cheated the Inland Revenue, and so there was no harm in his having a little on the side. I know two blacks do not make a white, but mercy is often called for in life, both for ourselves and others. If you have sacked someone because you have been robbed, or if there has been gross misconduct or disobedience, you do not need by law to give wages in lieu of notice, provided you can prove it. If you cannot prove it, you could be forced, by court action, to pay damages for unjust dismissal. Either way, my view is to give the wages necessary and pack the person off quietly.

Whatever you do, do not accuse a thief in public or before witnesses, otherwise you may find yourself in trouble. Some thieves are also barrack-room lawyers and could cost you a lot in legal cases for slander, etc.

Vindictiveness is not a very Christian attitude anyway, and it is better for the thief to pass out of your life unless the amount was extremely large. Perhaps his own conscience is sufficient punishment.

References and Testimonials

It is easy to give a good testimonial. A good employee should be offered one on leaving, and the wise employee will accept it, with a few photocopies, for sending out to prospective employers should the need arise.

The testimonial can be given in the old-fashioned way; a list of facts, headed by the words 'To Whom It May Concern'. The sort of thing that is common for a fairly useless worker is the one given on page 69. It is a good example of the usual piffle that no-one reads, being trite and dull. If you want to give a really good reference, cut out the 'To Whom It May Concern' and simply write something like this:

'Whoever employs Mr. J. E. Brown will be lucky. He is a man who knows his job and pays attention to it. But he is more than that. In the six years he has served us he has been careful, willing and keen. Everyone in our organization is sad because he is going – which is putting it mildly', or

'Miss Joan Smith is a girl in a hundred. She is delightful to work with and in the four years she has been with us has not only done her own job superbly but shown loyalty and intelligence to a high degree. She ran our publicity department single-handed, and also took charge of the sales department when the writer was abroad on business. Whatever she does is carried out to the best of her considerable ability. Miss Smith possesses integrity, common-sense, organizing ability, speed and resourcefulness rarely found in one so young.' This is of course an excellent testimonial and cannot be given to the ordinary worker.

Whatever you do, keep testimonials brief, bright, and to the point.

In the instance of a very bad worker, you can refuse to give a testimonial, although this is a hard line to take. Kinder, perhaps, is to give a simple recital of any good points, however few.

For the dishonest person, or somebody who has been really useless, the diplomatic reply to a request for a reference is that you will provide one to any firm who writes for it.

One hopes that this will be the end of the matter. You would presume that such an employee would not refer anyone to you, but from my experience they sometimes do. It is then that great care is required owing to the legal risk. Possibly you are best to answer very, very shortly on the telephone. If you have to write, your reply should be marked 'Strictly confidential', and the, envelope also. Your letter thus becomes what is called 'privileged', and so long as it is accurate and not malicious a great deal can be said. It should be addressed to the partner, if it is a partnership, or to the chairman, director, or secretary, if a limited company. The secretary is best unless you know the director's name. In such instances, as so often in life, it is wise to say little. For example, 'We are afraid we cannot recommend the person named in your enquiry.'

Note that I have omitted his name so that if the letter is left lying about, it incriminates no individual.

Many employers prefer to 'phone you for a reference. This saves time and is of course one of the best ways of getting the facts. For a good worker it is easy. For an enquiry about a thief or about a person who has misbehaved, once again, say little. You never know who might be listening in at the other end. Just say, 'We do not recommend him,' or 'We let him go because we did not like him.'

Life is not easy for wrong-doers, nor for the foolish.

7

COSTING AND PRICING

Here is the formula.

Cost plus profit equals selling price.

Simple, isn't it?

It is no part of the purpose of this book to tell you how much you should add on for profit. This figure varies widely from trade to trade, and indeed from district to district within the same type of business, according to the strength of the competition.

What is essential is for you to decide on some fixed level of profit to be applied, a level which is realistic in terms of your being able to get enough business at that percentage margin, and then to stick to it accurately. This is by no means as simple as it may sound.

Of course it is easy to know that you can buy, for example, a widget for £1 or that you can buy a dozen widgets for £10.

You might think that, if you were a shop-keeper, and you could sell 10 widgets every month at £1·50 each, then you would be making a profit of £5 a month on widgets. Alas, this is far from the truth. Do not forget that your costs must also include your overheads, and in the case of a shop-keeper, these will at least include rates, rent, light, heat, postage, telephone, advertising, and an accumulation of many other things like insurance and sundry expenses which together add up to a very great deal. In order to arrive at the true cost of buying your goods, you have to include for an extra percentage of 'overheads' before you can see what your real profit is. These overheads will probably decrease percentagewise as the volume going through your business increases, which is one of the so-called 'advantages of scale'.

The best way to arrive at a satisfactory figure for these hidden costs is to examine your previous year's profit and loss account, and see what percentage of your total turnover these hidden costs were. Then you must add on this percentage to your cost price, before adding on your profit to arrive at a proper selling price.

In the case of businesses which quote prices for doing particular jobs, the procedure might well be a little different. Supposing you were a small builder. Suppose you employed six men and had a small office. Each man works for 250 days a year (knocking off 115 days for weekends and holidays) so each man-day worked costs, in addition to wages and material, one fifteen hundredth of your annual overheads. So if you quote for a job which is going to take three men five days to carry out, that is fifteen man days, so you must add one per cent of your total annual overheads in order to arrive at a true cost for the job. This is in addition to the cost of wages, National Insurance, materials, and sub-contrators' bills. Only when this grand total has been added up should you add on the extra percentage for your own profits.

In calculating the cost of your overheads, do not forget to include for inflation. All these costs seem to rise year by year, often at a very high rate, and there is generally no sense in doing business at a loss. If there is deflation, the reverse would be true.

Orders at a Loss

The exception is when a businessman has to take orders either for no profit, or even at a small loss for special reasons. Returning to our small builder, perhaps he has three important jobs coming up later in the summer, but in the meantime has nothing for his workmen to do. Rather than lay them off, he might prefer to quote a very competitive price for a job which will take them through the slack period, or perhaps he wants to compete because he believes the customer is going to provide further work if he is satisfied with the first job. There is often method in the madness. However, too many losses result in ruin, so they are only to be indulged in for exceptional reasons and rarely.

Your Rate of Profit

The fact that you always price in a rate of profit which you have calculated to be adequate does not mean that you have earned a living at the end of the year. Such reasons as the following may have prevented you:

(a) insufficient turnover;
(b) bad debts;
(c) claims for which you were not insured;
(d) personal ill-health.

There are, therefore, times when it is possible and desirable to get a little extra profit. This may particularly apply to small jobs, or where some geographical advantage is on your side, as, for instance, a building firm where the site is very near the yard, or where a good stock of bricks, tiles and timber at a lower price than normal was being held.

Conversely, it may sometimes be necessary to cut your margin of profit to secure good orders, especially if the customer is known to be a quick payer. In short, your priority is to be flexible and indeed that is one of the secrets of success for the small business. The small business always scores over the bigger one in terms of instant adjustment to new conditions and flexibility of operation. However, the smaller business normally requires more good profit orders because the turnover is smaller.

In manufacturing business, the profit can frequently depend on the number of items produced, or on the possibility of buying a better machine which will produce large quantities.

A very good example of this is publishing a book. With a paper-back like the one you are reading, the cost of starting it up, i.e. setting up the type, getting proofs, making corrections, designing the cover, etc., come to as much as the cost of printing about 15,000 copies. However, the cost of printing the books once the machine is going is relatively cheap, and for this reason an edition of 15,000 copies costs about 30% more per copy than an edition of 30,000 copies. Very nice, thanks, if you can sell 30,000. But what if you sell only 15,000, and get stuck with the rest?

This type of equation applies to all sorts of manufacturing businesses, and it is just these kinds of things that make costing and business so difficult.

For all these reasons, your costing must be done with an eye on the whole picture. So must your buying. It is no use buying goods which you cannot sell, and which you subsequently have to dispose of at a loss. On the other hand, it is equally useless to buy so few that you have to pay high prices and your goods are not competitive with similar ones offered by other operators. If you cannot sell a particular line in sufficient quantities to make an adequate profit, it is probably not worth carrying that line.

Inflation

Inflation is one of the biggest bug-bears to affect modern business. It is a term which is often misused, but really means a general fall in the value of money, in terms of the goods and services that money will purchase.

Contrary to general belief, inflation is caused neither by Trade Unions nor by Capitalists, nor is it caused by property 'speculators'. It is in general caused by Governments, who seek for electoral reasons to allow people to have more money than they have really earned, and compensate for this by reducing the value of that money. Because inflation now seems to be such an established feature of business life all over the world, it is right that a small section of this book should be devoted to explaining how you, as a small businessman, can avoid the worst effects of it. The main ways in which the process of inflation can affect your business are as follows:

(1) The cost of goods, services, or wages may rise between the time you quote for a job and the time you carry it out. The way to avoid this is not to quote for jobs until the work is imminent, and then to make the best possible allowance for this. In the case of contracts which are to be carried out over a long period, it may be possible to include escalator clauses in the contract which enable you to increase the price according to some fixed indicator, such as the Retail Price Index, or the actual increases in costs that you have suffered.

(2) When you sell or use goods which you have in stock, you find that the amount of money that you get for them is not sufficient to replace those stocks for future customers. In this way, you find that you are constantly having to inject new capital into the business in order to maintain a constant turnover in real terms. Also, at the end of the year, you have to value your stock and work in progress, and where this exceeds the value of the stock and work in progress at the beginning of the year, the difference may be taxed as though it was profit. This process of inflation and taxation is steadily undermining the real capital of business. In order not to let it affect you, you must be extremely rigorous in keeping your stocks to the minimum that is necessary to conduct the business properly, and you must probably increase the selling price of your existing stocks whenever the price from your suppliers goes up, if this is legal. As far as the end of the year is concerned, you must be quite ruthless in writing down the value of bad stock and work in progress. Although Governments in recent years have recognised this problem by allowing some element of 'stock relief' for larger companies, neglect of this precaution can still mean overvaluing stock which you may never

sell at its full price, and you will certainly be paying tax earlier than you need to. Be guided in this matter by your accountant. (3) In inflationary times, staff expect their wages or salaries to rise at a level at least which will keep pace with rises in the cost of living. For this reason, it is necessary (provided it is not prohibited by Government edict) to review at more frequent intervals the pay of staff, particularly important staff, otherwise they may become dissatisfied and leave. By failing to increase wages and salaries, you rapidly fall behind those offered by other people in the locality. Conversely, of course, where you have staff who are not really pulling their weight, it is possible to keep their wages or salaries the same, and their take-home pay in real terms will fall. At least it is nicer than having to reduce their wages!

Buying

I was brought up in the belief that you cannot sell what you have not got, and that a thing well bought is half sold. These are true and good maxims, but deserve some qualification. The vital thing for the new businessman is either to possess or else to acquire the knowledge which will enable him to buy at the correct terms. To obtain the best discounts, three things are usually necessary:

    (*a*) to buy from the correct supplier
    (*b*) to buy a minimum quantity
    (*c*) to pay by a certain date.

Sometimes it is wise to buy the minimum necessary for the largest discount, but this is no good if it means buying more than your customers can absorb, or so much that it will deteriorate or remain on your hands for long periods. In this instance, you may have to be content with less at a smaller discount.

As far as suppliers are concerned, it is important not to get into a rut and continue dealing always with the same people, regardless of the competition. Things change the whole time, and new suppliers who may also have new products for you to sell, are constantly coming into the picture. Therefore check your purchasing from time to time to see if there are others who could supply you more cheaply, or with goods of a better quality at the same price.

Many firms allow settlement discounts of one kind or another. Common is $2\frac{1}{2}\%$ for payment within a certain period, e.g. 7 days. Usually it is worth trying to secure this.

Don't Gamble as Yet

With your early buying, I do urge you to avoid gambling. You are embarking on an enterprise which I assume means risking your all, as well as perhaps many thousands of pounds belonging to other people, so this is not the time for 'long shots'.

Some suppliers will offer what seem to be extremely advantageous discounts for large quantities. Bargain snatching is, of course, always wise if you know that you can sell everything you buy. When you are starting up, however, this cannot be the case. At this stage you still have to get the feel of your market. It may easily be that in a month or two you will realize that you can sell several hundred of the item being offered, and then you can take advantage of the offer. Until you have more experience, it is better to settle for the small quantity.

In most types of business, there are many different items to be stocked, and all of these tie up your capital. Also, once the market for a particular product is filled, sales are apt to diminish or stop unless this is an item which people repeat frequently.

Therefore take time to work out a plan and do not be rushed into high risks. Be conservative. Avoid trying new ideas which experienced people have not experimented with. They probably know – they may not – but you have plenty of time to consider pioneering and risking things once you have built up a bit of capital and profit.

Stock Control

Some method of stock control is essential otherwise you cannot know how many you are selling of any particular product. Basically, there are two methods which are appropriate for different types of business. Where you are selling a wide range of different products which each sell perhaps only one or two per month, then probably the best method is to attach some kind of tag to the item (this is particularly suitable for the jewellery trade) and remove this when the item is sold. Put the tags in the till. If you write the date of purchase on the tag, then you can see how long it has taken for the item to sell and you can decide whether it is worth buying again. With this system you would be re-ordering quite quickly but in fairly small quantities, and it may well be worth your while to use one wholesaler or distributor rather than trying to buy direct from many different manufacturers.

The alternative method of stock control is to check over all the stock at stated intervals, and keep a record of how many there were and how many you bought. This method is common to most of the large multiple shops. In order for this to work properly, for items of slow turnover I would say that the stocks had to be checked at least once a month. Far more often if turnover is fast. The important thing is to turf out lines which do not sell enough to be worth stocking, to reduce the quantities held in stock of those items which are not turning over fast enough, and, most important of all, to increase the quantity ordered of an item which has sold out. Thus, if you buy a particular widget, and check the stock at the end of each month, supposing at the end of the first month you find that the six that you had bought had all gone, you do not buy six more, you buy twelve. If at the end of the next month, these twelve have all gone, you go on increasing the quantity until you hit the ceiling, i.e. until you have got to the quantity where there are some left. Only in that way can you find out what the full potential of the widget is.

Establish a target figure (I cannot suggest one because different trades vary so much) of the number of times per year that you want your stock to turn over. Supposing you decide that eight times a year is the appropriate figure. In that case, you would check your stock every month and you would reckon to make up the quantities to the amount that you can sell in six weeks, each time. In addition to this you may need to allow a lead-time for delays in delivery. Of course, in many types of business, and especially with perishable goods, the stock will need to be checked more often. An example of a stock control system is given in the appendix. (Page 118.)

8

SALES AND PUBLICITY

Earlier, I said you cannot sell what you have not got. It is equally true that you are not likely to sell what the public does not know exists. Nor will you sell it if the public does not know you've got it, or if the public does not know you are there. Whether you have a business with a hundred representatives or agents throughout the world, or just a tiny back-street shop which you opened in your spare time, the same truth applies.

Compared with some countries, I am afraid that we British are apt to forget salesmanship, marketmanship, and packaging. Remember that the mass of the public are not able to be an expert on every product that they buy. For this reason, more and more people are buying inferior products simply because they are better packaged. Of course, we know that quality tells in the end, but if your packaging and sales are good, quality can tell for you from the start.

Provided you have the right goods, do get them attractively and colourfully presented and displayed. Even if your business is one that sells only services or something that you cannot show, you still have to sell yourself. Therefore take care that you are neat, tidy, and up-to-date in your appearance. Until you are established, it is very important what you look like. Once you are rich and famous, you can afford to go around looking like an eccentric.

Many men fail in business because they neglect or despise salesmanship. Some may regard it as slightly beneath them, others, more commonly, do not understand its importance. Fix this, therefore, in your mind. In business, ruin faces those who do not attend to marketing.

As an army 'marches on its stomach', a business marches on its sales, whether these be of goods or services. No business will flourish if salesmanship and the attitude that goes with it stagnate. Lack of orders, of contracts, or of work, hold up everything. You must have output if you are to have profit. Large turnover can be the quick way to big profits.

The Repeat Order

The repeat order is what you thrive on over the years. Sometimes it may be worth getting the first order at a very low or nil profit, if you are sure that the repeat orders from the customer are going to be substantial. If you can demonstrate that you know and understand the products or services that you offer, and build up a feeling of mutual trust between you and your customer, then the repeat orders will flow in. The man who knows the job usually wins. So, through your knowledge, guide and help your customers to ensure that they remain customers and friends.

Why Knowhow Pays

I will quote three examples. In a slightly dark cupboard of our home, we discovered that the floor appeared to be damp over an area of several square feet. We feared that this might cause rot, and contacted a builder. He examined it and said, 'That is not wet and it will not rot. What has happened is that maybe 20 or 30 years ago, someone spilt grease or oil on the floor, and the mark has remained.' To our expression of surprise and doubt, he remarked, 'Don't believe me, prove it yourself. Heat an iron and place it on the area and you will find that the grease melts. Also, if it is damp, it will spread, so draw a pencil line round the outline of the 'damp' and check up every month to see if it extends.'

That was 20 years ago, and he has been proved right.

Later we found a crack in a wall behind some old wallpaper. This was about a quarter of an inch wide, and as we looked at it daily it seemed to be widening.

With visions of the wall falling in, we 'phoned the builder to ask if it was dangerous. 'Yes,' he said, 'It could be. Are you sure it is getting wider?' As we were not certain, he said, 'Well, make sure – stick a few pieces of sticky paper across the gap. If they break inside a week, phone me.' That was ages ago, and the sticky paper is still intact.

The third problem was where a rat made a hole through a cement floor into a building. 'Take a handful of cement, break a bottle into small pieces, and cement the hole up with lots of the glass protruding through the other side of the cement into the hole. You will never see the rat again.'

This builder could have earned a few pounds by doing something to the hole in the floor or doing something to the crack in the wall, but how much wiser he was not to. What he did was to prove (*a*) his knowledge, and (*b*) his integrity.

Was it surprising that when I had a new warehouse to build costing thousands of pounds, I entrusted the work to this knowledgeable man?*

The above is better salesmanship than the high-pressure American types. The examples given are exceptionally good, but the same sort of opportunity arises in all kinds of day to day affairs, from the voluntary cleaning of the windscreen at a petrol station, a special order for a book by a bookseller or some larger favour you may do for a customer. All are salesmanship of a high order.

How to Lose Custom

Some time ago I was considering buying an expensive lawn mower. I asked if it was possible for me to see one in action, suggesting that perhaps the shop had sold one to a person nearby who might be willing for me to go and watch it while he was using it. I also asked whether the makers ever gave a demonstration. The reply was, 'I suppose you would like us to come and cut your lawn – well, we won't.'

Needless to say I did not buy my lawn mower from that shop.

Of course the customer is not always right and occasionally you may have to stand up to him, but do remember that he usually has the whip hand, and in business one quarrels with customers at the peril of one's bread and butter. Particularly if you are running a shop or a local trade, do not forget that people discuss local matters with their friends, and by upsetting one influential person you could lose yourself dozens, or even hundreds of orders.

It costs nothing to be courteous and obliging, and it normally helps business. If you respect your customers, they will respect you. Of course there is always the occasional bully who may try to take advantage of you, but these people are probably well-known in the locality and there is little to be lost by having nothing to do with them.

Praise your goods or services, without making exaggerated claims. Make sure that your wares are shown and known, and

---

*Kingswood Building Number One, Kingswood, Surrey, built by William Matthews & Son, Hooley, Surrey. The home of Elliot Right Way Books.

remember that a satisfied customer, or a good job of work well done are above the best advertisements.

Get Your Own Publicity

There is nothing more important, but there are so many ways of doing this that one could hardly enumerate them all. I shall mention a few of the more useful. Later on, when your concern has grown to a large size, it might possibly pay to call in skilled experts. At the beginning, for the sake of economy, you must endeavour to do your own publicity. The type of advertising or publicity in which you will indulge depends entirely upon the type of business and perhaps on whether it is a new business or one that you have taken over. Obtaining publicity for an established business may mean little more than improving the existing methods. In the case of a new business, a different plan is likely to be required. Analyse your answers to the following questions;

(1) Who is likely to benefit by the goods or services that you have to offer?

(2) Within what area will it be profitable for you to trade?

(3) How much money dare you allocate?

(4) What season of the year is it wisest for you to launch the publicity?

(5) Which are the best media to use: press, local papers, personal canvassing, hoardings, shop notice boards, etc.?

All the above need consideration in relation to your own problem. Not knowing what type of business you are engaged in, all I can give you here is general remarks and advice.

The 'Pilot' Scheme

In all advertising or publicity, particularly if you are inexperienced, a trial scheme is essential. In this way you can check whether it is going to be worthwhile to continue spending money on a particular method. By the trial scheme, I mean something like this. Suppose you have started a small decorating business and you want to announce it to people within a radius of five miles of your district. Perhaps the best method of doing this would be by personal call. I put this first because there is normally no better way to get business. For your trial area you could select one street or streets, and start calling at all the houses or business premises. This is a simple form of trial, because if you obtain results you will have started to do business before you know where you are. Later on you may find yourself so busy that you have not time to do these personal calls, and it may be necessary to engage perhaps some retired person or part-time worker on your behalf. Don't overlook part-time married women – some make excellent travellers.

Leaflet Method

Where personal canvassing is unsuitable for your trade, a trial can be carried out with an inexpensive leaflet or catalogue. The method is to select a street or streets and have your publicity material delivered to all the houses and business premises. This test enables you to avoid expense if the scheme fails. If a reasonably good response is received, the method can be extended to cover whatever area you feel is suitable, and you might spend more money on producing a better leaflet.

The same type of pilot scheme could be arranged with press advertising. Display or classified advertisements can be inserted in one of the local newspapers, and the results watched carefully before embarking on larger advertisements or a national scheme, or before even repeating the original advertisement.

Do not forget that many businesses have ruined themselves by too much advertising. Beware.

Speaking from thousands of pounds worth of bitter experience, I do not believe the experts who tell me that where at first you don't succeed, constant repetition will get results. My own experience has nearly always been that the first insertion is the one that pays the best. Subsequent advertising usually yields a deteriorating return. And don't, please, believe the nonsense that advertising and public relations consultants may tell you about the value of 'white space'. It can be valuable, but it costs just as much as space filled with print. If you buy a space in a newspaper, fill it with your message. Mail order advertisers know exactly how their advertisement pays, and you hardly ever see them wasting space.

It is good advice to freshen up your copy from time to time, and, if you are doing any sort of mail order business, use some sort of key as a check on result. For instance, you could insert a department number, or a slight change in your address, as people who are writing to you will copy what they see when addressing the envelope.

If you are giving a telephone number, which is usually a wise thing to do, then ask where the customer saw the advertisement and make a note for your research.

The Telephone

For some reason the telephone in Great Britain is neglected as a means of introducing yourself to possible customers. However, in relation to the cost and time occupied, this is probably one of the best media. Care has to be taken in timing, for if you ring someone to enquire whether they want any decorating at 8 o'clock in the morning, you are liable to get a snub. But if you choose a suitable time, the difference of the idea might impress.

The Publicity Secret

The secret of good advertising or publicity is to get yourself or your product talked about.

You must make a study of the particular target which you have in mind, and then devise some method relative to the goods or service you offer, to make your name a household word in the district. Then you have done something which should bring in business.

I remember the early days when F. W. Woolworth & Company sold nothing over six(old)pence. I am quite sure that it was one of their own publicity experts who started the story of the piano department in the Aberdeen branch, and of course many of us can remember the excellent buckets they used to sell for sixpence. They probably didn't make anything on the buckets, but secured their profit on other items that people put into the buckets before leaving the shop. In pre-war days, there was another joke circulating, which asked why, if you were found standing on a sixpence, you would resemble F. W. Woolworth's? And the answer was, 'Nothing over sixpence'. Wonderful free publicity, the joke.

Window Cards

Most local newsagents and some other shops have a notice-board in or near their window where you can put a postcard advertisement for a few pence a week. These have the advantage of cheapness and locality, and people do read them. Use all suitable sites in your area. Don't just copy the other cards. Make your card different, even if the only difference is the use of bright coloured paper or a red or green ink to paint a frame around your message. Here is the sort of thing.

```
            J. W. TIBBET

            4, NEW STREET

             HALMBURY

            Tel. 6101

               for

Electrical Installations, Re-wiring,
Appliance Servicing and
Installations, TV and Radio Repairs


Free Estimates          Phone any time
```

9

ETIQUETTE, GOODWILL, AND BUSINESS CUSTOM

People who start businesses do so from all sorts of different backgrounds. One may have 20 years' experience with good firms, and will know most of the answers to the problems of what to do and what is not done.

Others, however, will only have the vaguest notions of this subject, and may well have come from a completely non-business background. Of course, business etiquette is based on good manners, but even with these and an ample supply of commonsense, there are some things worth mentioning.

Don't Run Down Your Competitors

Many people think it is clever to go about making derogatory remarks regarding competitors, and perhaps even boasting about how much better they can do. Nowhere is it more true to say that pride often goes before a fall than in competitive business. To adopt an attitude of slanging one's competitors is the almost certain way towards trouble, if not disaster. From a commonsense angle, it is well to realize that many customers will have been dealing with your competitors for generations and hold them in high regard. For all you know they may be very friendly with them, so that any disparaging remarks coming from you could be repeated to the competitors concerned.

As a new entry into a trade, probably with very limited resources, it is folly to invite the power of your competitors against you. A strong competitor may adopt a policy against you which could ruin you.

It is, therefore, wise to try and keep all the goodwill you can even if it is from competitors.

Shortly after the turn of the century, before the advent of buses, a man used to drive a horse-trap which took eight or ten people for two or three miles from the railway station to their village.

He had done this for years, but with the internal combustion engine, a competitor entered the field running a small bus.

The horse-owner was so angry that he started condemning his competitor and there were many fierce arguments as to who had the right to take the passengers home. Finally the owner of the horse began throwing tacks and nails on the road to puncture the tyres of the motor vehicle. You can probably imagine the end of this story, which was a court case, and finally the cab driver had to give up his business. He was too old to change with the times.

Similar situations can arise these days, with the accelerating advance of technological change. I urge you to move with the times rather than to slang your competitors. Usually in most industries and trades, there is ample room for everyone. Another danger of slanging your competitor is that if you said something slanderous about him or his goods, you could run a risk of a court case against you and this could be ruinously costly. Talk your own goods up, don't run the other fellow's down.

Your Word is Your Bond

Never endeavour to be too clever in business, because doing so is the surest way to lose goodwill. Carry out your promises. Keep to yourself all confidences which are reposed in you. Few newcomers to business realize the importance of this hidden factor of goodwill. Goodwill is perhaps the greatest asset of any business.

Don't Be a 'Smart Alec'

There will be many occasions when you have to quote a price, and in doing so you are of course fully entitled to protect yourself by a variety of clauses in your quotation as mentioned earlier in the book (page 63), such as the following:

'Subject to the goods being unsold.'

'Subject to labour or material costs not rising.'

'Subject to acceptance within two weeks.'

Never try to take advantage of these clauses, rather the other way.

An occasion may arise where through delay in acceptance, it becomes impossible to fulfil the contract at the original price. Provided you have covered yourself for such an eventuality, by all means ask for whatever is necessary to be added to the quotation. The point I am making, however, is never use such conditions merely to enable you to secure extra advantage, otherwise goodwill suffers. Similarly, by falling in line with a customer's wish wherever you can, in circumstances such as those outlined above, it is likely to be to your credit for the future. Customers are people like ourselves, and some of them have long memories. If you have been honest with someone, or treated them well, they are likely to remember it, and you are likely to get the repeat orders which are the secret of long-term success.

Avoid Threats

Some business people go around making what might be called polite threats. Sometimes these are genuine, but often they are tricks to try and obtain business. This sort of thing:

> 'If you don't accept now we will be sold out.'
> 'You have never been offered such a bargain in your life.'
> 'Take it or leave it.'
> 'This is the last one.'

Be careful that what you say is right, but also try to avoid the old-fashioned 'Pistol-at-the-head' method, because it is one that is employed normally by crooked people and not by responsible firms. There will of course be occasions when you have to make a quotation subject to a reply by a certain date owing to supplies being genuinely limited, etc., but wherever you have to put such stipulations in, try to put them in a straightforward form without using any implied threats. People resent it. They feel they are being rushed into a decision which should involve a lot of thought.

Ultimatums

It might almost be said that the good businessman never uses ultimatums. There may be the odd exception, but normally avoid this kind of thing:

> 'Reply in 24 hours or else.'
> 'Otherwise we will close our account with you.'
> 'This is your last chance.'
> 'Either increase your discount or tell your representative never to call again.'

The ultimatum is often something said or written in anger,

when judgement is apt to be faulty. I have seen many people having to eat their words, which if they had been more discreet they would never have had to do. The traveller at whom today you shout, 'Never call again,' may next month have got a job with your best suppliers, and then he may try to be vindictive and create difficulties for you.

Disagreements

Endeavour to avoid quarrels, because none of us know what the future holds. This brings me back to the question of maintaining goodwill, and creating it. Let me illustrate what can happen.

We once had a most insolent customer, a man who practically never bought from us, but used to put us to endless trouble to give him quotations. The firm I was with at the time were agreeable to do this. For a year or two we sent estimates of the lowest price. Then we learnt indirectly that he was placing his orders with one of our competitors with whom he played golf. Our research discovered that he was also giving us bogus enquiries just to find out information and pass on the prices to his friends. Our firm was a powerful one, and after about two years, we decided that this person had taken us for a long enough ride, and it was time to end it. From thenceforward, we gradually increased our quotations to him, not quoting him the lowest price, but something higher, so as to deny him valuable market information. For two or three years he did not spot what we were doing, and over a period of time, owing to the fact that he was not guided by our true prices, he placed his orders with our competitors at too high a price. In the end he found himself landed with a lot of merchandise bought in the wrong market, and he was practically ruined. Outwitted at his own game.

Free Service

Many people in business adopt a grasping attitude and try to get the highest price for everything on all occasions. Unfortunately for them, the way to make the most money is not necessarily always to get the highest price.

Customers are human, and the urge to find and secure bargains is keen. To try to run a business, as many people do, on what might be called a very strict costing basis, frequently ends in disaster, particularly for the new entry who has his way to make.

In business one normally has to allow one's head to rule the heart, but there are times when it can pay handsomely to do the opposite.

In other words, if you have secured a bargain supply of merchandise, pass some of this bargain on to your customers, if not all of it. This is one of the tricks of making business friends, and while one must avoid giving away all one's advantage, to do so occasionally creates goodwill and wonderful publicity.

The Bait

Big stores and similar concerns use what are called loss leaders. What happens is this. The concern buys a bargain lot of something, and then promotes and sells it at perhaps the price they paid, possibly even at a slight loss, but certainly on a much reduced profit percentage. They do this in order to draw customers into their stores and warehouses. Then they hope the customers will buy other things. For the small concern I don't think it is wise to sell at a loss unless you have to, but if you can put forward one or two bargains in the list of goods you sell, these often go far towards securing other profitable business. Bargain items are especially good to use when trying to open accounts with good customers. Low prices speak louder than words.

Good Manners Help

Finally, when someone 'phones up or calls in, do remember that a nice welcome is attractive. I once knew a man whose work entailed negotiating with a number of official bodies, and who was known to be successful in getting favourable decisions after others had failed. His success was based on simply understanding human nature and being courteous.

In your business, welcome people on the 'phone and try to make them feel important because they are customers. Similarly, in your letters try to bring in a certain amount of friendliness. I do not suggest either flattery or welcome to the extent of dishonesty. For instance, if you are having difficulty with someone, it is insincere to flatter him at the same time. But in all normal dealings you will find kindness and courtesy will do much to help make your business profitable.

Avoid too much old-fashioned formality in your letters. If you know someone as Mr. Brown, don't write to him as 'Dear Sir,'. 'Dear Mr. Brown' is warmer without being familiar.

Complaints

Recently I got a letter like this from a stranger in Edinburgh:

Dear Sir,

I have always understood the price of your books is 75p, but I have just bought one on fishing from a shop in Princes Street which has a 95p ticket on it. All I want to know is whether it is correct, or if I have been swindled. Let me hasten to add that I thought the book excellent value at 95p.

Yours sincerely,

. . . .

I could have replied:

Dear Sir,

Since November 30th, the price of our book was advanced to 95p, which please note.

Yours faithfully,

. . . .

Instead I wrote:

Dear Sir,

As one Scotsman to another I congratulate you on taking the trouble to write to us which so few people do. I am pleased to say that your Booksellers are honest people. Yes, I am sorry that we were forced to raise the price of our books to 95p owing to rapidly increasing costs. As you may know, books have to be printed in very large numbers at a time, and kept in publishers' warehouses for a period of months, if not years. With rapidly increasing inflation, the time comes when prices get completely out of date in relation to current costs, and we find that we are not getting enough money in from the books we sell even to reprint them. For this reason, it is sometimes necessary to raise the price already printed on a book. It really is a case of putting the price up or going out of business.

I enclose our new catalogue, and on the back you will notice five other fishing books, some of which may be of interest to you. The booksellers in Princes Street normally keep all these in stock.

With assurance of our best service.

Yours faithfully,

. . . .

10

INSURANCE

Sometimes experienced business people make errors regarding their insurance. This is easier in times of rapid inflation. It is essential for the businessman to see that his stocks of goods, property, and work in progress, are fully insured. Usually, they need to be insured at the replacement cost value.

Among other items of insurance which must be carefully considered is to insure your employees against accident, and to insure against public liability. The former is now required by law in Great Britain.

Insurance agents and companies will be able to help you on these questions, but do remember that the majority of them are anxious to sell you as much insurance as possible, and some of this may not be necessary. In general, I make a rule never to insure anything that I can afford to lose. Where the risk represents any serious part of my capital, then I know it is wise to cover it fully. Of course you may have a comprehensive policy which covers practically everything, and there may not be much saving by seeking to exclude small items. By carrying the first £XXX of loss yourself (if you can afford to) you can often save greatly on the premium.

Life Insurance

People take different views of this, but I think it is very straightforward.

The self-employed businessman in the U.K. only has a limited entitlement to the State pension scheme, and he does not get a pension from his employer. If, therefore, he wants to be secure in his old age, he has either got to save up enough capital to live on, or else he has got to take out an insurance policy to provide him with a pension. As rates of inflation rise, it is exceedingly difficult for an Insurance Company to offer a guarantee that the pension will be worth, in terms of real spending power, anything like the amount that is envisaged at the outset. Remember that policies that seem to promise a fantastic pension or a staggering cash sum on retirement are dealing with a date which is probably very many years ahead, but in the meantime the erosion in the value of money will have taken away a large part of, if not all of the value of those benefits.

Perhaps you are thinking of selling the business on retirement, and in this case it could well be that the money you get can be considered as a nest-egg for your retirement. Quite separate from this in a way, yet usually combined with it by Life Insurance Companies, is the matter of protection for your widow or children in the event of your early demise. Here again, the rate of inflation can enter calculations, but what you are considering is a matter of chance which can be arrived at by an actuarial calculation. The independent businessman frequently has a large part of his capital tied up in the business, and of course in some kinds of business it would be possible for a widow to realise a substantial sum of money if the owner died. However, in other kinds of business, where there is perhaps little stock or goodwill, the value may be negligible or even nothing. An insurance policy can be taken out to provide a lump sum at death for your wife or dependants, for a fairly small premium. If your own house is mortgaged, it is also possible for you to take out a mortgage protection policy which would enable the outstanding loan to be paid off at your death. This one is almost certainly essential, otherwise your dependents would have to sell the house in order to repay the debt.

In general, however, be guided by the fact that most of us pay out in real terms far more in insurance than we ever get back. You have only got to look at the beautiful offices and enormous buildings that the insurance companies own to be sure of that.

11

BUSINESS TERMS, PHRASES AND ABBREVIATIONS

The use of many expressions and terms current in business is, outside certain well-defined limits, to be depreciated. It becomes, in fact, one of those forms of laziness of which we are all guilty.

One of the problems is that different terms apply in different parts of the country or world, even in the same trade, and confusion is likely to arise if some abbreviations are used. This underlines a very important rule: Make sure that everything you write is clear.

The letters 'E. & O.E.' are seen on quotations, invoices, etc., and stand for an important safeguard: *Errors and omissions excepted*. Curiously enough, they are not so often seen today, and I personally deplore their absence as they provide an honourable retreat in the event of a blunder.

C.I.F. stands for *Cost, Insurance and Freight*. If I ask a merchant in America to quote me for one ton of cotton, c.i.f. Liverpool, his price to me includes the cost of the cargo, the insurance and the freight – the last two of which he pre-pays. Delivery would be alongside the dock at Liverpool. Unloading charges would be my concern or – to use another business phrase – 'for my account'.

F.O.R. means *Free on Rail*, that is, free delivery as far as the *consignor's* railway station or depot.

F.O.B.: *Free on Board*, that is, delivered to the ship.

B/L: *Bill of Lading*, that is, a Bill of Authority for shipping merchandise by steamer.

Dy and d/d: Mean *delivery* and *delivered*, but these words should be written out in full.

Bulk delivery: Delivery only in large quantities.

Each trade has, of course, a host of expressions applicable to its own business, and whilst I do not intend to deal with the hundreds of specialised terms in this book, here is a list of a few of them together with foreign phrases which may be met:

LIST OF SOME TERMS USED IN BUSINESS

A/c.	Account.
Ack.	Acknowledge.
Addendum.	An additional remark to be added.
Ad fin.	Near or towards the end.
Ad hoc.	For this purpose.
Ad infinitum.	To infinity.
Ad lib. (ad libitum).	As much as you like; without control.
Ad modum.	Following the manner.
Ad referendum.	For further consideration.
Ad valorem. (A/V).	Based on value – sometimes a Customs & Excise term (or an import duty).
A.M.	Air Mail.
Amende honorable.	Satisfactory apology or reparation.
Antedate.	Dated earlier than arranged.
A/R.	All risks.
Argumenti causa.	For argument.
B/d.	Brought down (accounts).
B/E.	Bill of Exchange; also Bill of Entry (the latter for Customs).
B/f.	Brought forward (accounts).
B.H.P.	Brake Horse Power (Engineering).
B/L.	Bill of Lading.
Bleed.	The part of an illustration which runs off the page. (Printing.)
B.M.	British Monomark. (Bench Mark in the Ordnance Survey.)
B.T.U.	British Thermal Unit (heat).
B.W.G.	British Wire Gauge. (Engineering.)
C.A.	Chartered Accountant.
C. & F.	Cost and freight.
Carr. pd.	Carriage paid.
Casus belli.	Cause or justification of war.
Causa sine qua non.	An indispensable condition or cause.
Caveat emptor.	Let the buyer beware.
C/C.	Centre to Centre (measurement).
C.D. (Cum Dividend).	With the Dividend to come.

C/d.	Carried down (accounts).
Centum.	Per cent. (Used in cabling to save a word.)
Centistokes.	Measure of viscosity (analysis reports).
c/f.	Carried forward (accounts).
c.f.m.	Cubic feet per minute (engineering).
C.I.	Cast Iron.
C.I.F.	Cost, Insurance and Freight.
C.M.A.	Cash Monthly Account.
C/o.	Care of.
C.O.D.	Cash on delivery.
Contra.	Against; opposite (as 'Contra A/c').
Corrigendum.	Item, word or line to be corrected.
Cr.	Credit or Creditor.
C.S.	Cast Steel.
Cu.	Cubic.
C.W.O.	Cash with order.
D/d.	Delivered.
de facto.	In fact.
de jure.	By right.
Del credere.	Risk of a bad debt.
Distribute type.	'Break it down'. (Printing.)
Dr.	Debit or Debtor, or Doctor.
D.V. (Deo volente).	God willing.
D.V. & W.P.	God willing and weather permitting.
Dy.	Delivery.
E. & O.E.	Errors and Omissions Excepted.
e.g. (exempli gratia).	For example.
Electro.	Duplicate of type or block.
Et al.	And elsewhere.
Etc. (Etcetera).	And others.
Et seq.	And following.
Ex.	From (as 'ex stock').
Excl.	Exclusive or excluding.
Ex. div.	Exclusive of Dividend.
Ex officio.	By virtue of office.
Fait accompli.	An accomplished fact.
F.A.S.	Free alongside ship.
F.A.Q.	Fair average quality.
Fo.	Folio (accounts).

f.o.b.	Free on Board. ⎱ Buyer pays freight after
f.o.r.	Free on Rail. ⎰ put on ship or rail.
Force majeure.	Overriding circumstances, act of God, etc. (Whereby a contract may be cancelled or varied.)
Fount (or Font).	A set of type.
Ft.	Foot or feet.
Ft. cu.	Cubic foot or feet.
Ft. run.	Running feet – measurement of *length*.
ft. sup. or super.	Superficial feet – square measurement.
f.s.	Full size.
Galley proof.	Printer's proof before making into pages.
G.M.	Gun metal.
G.N.	Gross for nett – refers to bags only – pay on gross weight.
Hex. O. Hex.	Hexagonal-Round-Hexagonal. (Bolts and Nuts.)
i.e. (id est).	That is.
Inc.	Incorporated (U.S.A. equivalent of 'limited');
In extenso.	At full length.
In extremis.	At the extreme point.
In situ.	In position.
In status quo.	In the original state.
Inst.	Present month.
Inter alia.	Among other matters.
In toto.	In full.
In transitu.	On the way.
Inv.	Invoice.
I.O.U.	I owe you – a promise to repay money, the amount to be stated, signed but not dated.
Ipso facto.	By that very fact.
Laisser-faire.	To 'let it go' or leave it alone (thus, 'today's spirit of laisser-faire').
Lineal feet.	'Running' feet, in length, as distinct from square or superficial feet.
Ltd.	Limited.

Modus operandi.	Method of operation.
Mos.	Months.
M.P.G.	Miles per gallon.
M.P.H.	Miles per hour.
M.S.	Mild Steel. (Engineering.)
Ms. and mss.	Manuscript and manuscripts.
M.V.	Motor vessel.
Nem. con. (Nemine contradicente.)	Without opposition.
Ne plus ultra.	None better.
Non seq.	It does not follow.
Nulli secundus.	Second to none.
o/a.	On account; also over-all (measurement).
O/C.	Overcharge.
O/D.	Overdraft or overdrawn.
O.H.M.S.	On His/Her Majesty's Service.
Onus.	Responsibility.
%	Per cent or per hundred.
O.P.	Out of print.
O/R.	Owner's risk.
O/S.	Outstanding; also outsize.
P.A.	Per annum, yearly; also Personal Assistant.
p.c.	per centum; per hundred.
Per.	By.
Per diem.	By the day.
Persona gratia.	In personal favour.
P/L.	Profit and loss.
Pld.	Planed.
P.O.D.	Proof of delivery.
Post-date.	To date in advance – a later date.
p.p.	Per pro (on behalf of); also pages: (pp.)
P.P.M.	Parts per million (analysis).
Prima facie.	As far as first appears – on the face of it.
Pro.	For.
Pro forma.	As a matter of form. (Pro forma invoice, one calling for cash in advance.)
Pro rata.	Proportionately.
Pro tem.	For the time being.

Prox. (proximo).	Next month.
P.S.	Post scriptum – written afterwards; an afterthought.
P.S.I.	Per square inch.
Q.S.	Quantity small (recipes or analysis); also Quantity Surveyor.
Quid pro quo.	Equivalent compensation. 'Tit for tat.'
Qui vive.	Who is there? (Also used for 'on the alert'.)
Q.V. (Quod vide).	Which see.
R.C.	Reinforced concrete; also Roman Catholic.
R.D.	Refer to drawer (e.g. a cheque which a bank will not meet).
Rd.	Round.
Rep.	Representative.
R.P.M., or revs.	Revolutions per minute
R.S.J.	Rolled steel joist. (Constructional Engineering.)
R.S.V.P.	Please reply.
R.W.H.	Rainwater Head. (Building.)
R.W.P.	Rainwater Pipe. (Building.)
Seriatim.	Serially, one after the other.
Sine die.	Indefinitely.
Sine qua non.	A necessity.
Sq. or Sqre.	Square. (Also a timber measurement.)
Sq. Rd. Sq.	Square-Round-Square. (Bolts and Nuts.)
Status quo.	Existing condition.
Std.	Standard. (Also a timber measurement.)
Stereo (Stereotype).	Duplicate of a line block. (Printing.)
Stet.	Let it stand; leave as before.
Sub judice.	Under consideration, not yet settled in court.
S.W.G.	Standard Weight or Wire Gauge. (Eng.).
T. & G.	Tongued and grooved (timber).
T.G. & V.	Tongued, grooved and V-jointed (timber).
Tel. quel.	Quality offered just as it is.
Trs.	Transpose. (Proof reading.)

T.S.	Total solids. (Analysis reports.)
Ult. (ultimo).	Last month.
Ultra vires.	Beyond one's powers.
Va.	Volt amperes. (Also U.S.A. abbreviation for Virginia.)
Verbatim.	Word for word.
Verb sap.	A word to the wise is sufficient.
Via.	By way of.
Via media.	Between extremes.
Vice.	In place of.
Vice versa.	The other way round.
Vide.	See.
Vide infra.	See below.
Viva voce.	By word of mouth.
Viz.	Namely.
W/e.	Week-ending.
w.e.f.	With effect from.
W.F.I.	Wait for it.
W.G.	Wire gauge.
W.I.	Wrought Iron.
W.P.B.	Waste paper basket.
Wt.	Weight.
W/V.	Weight volume. (Analysis.)
W.W.P.	Water Waste Preventor. (Building.)
X.O.X.	Hexagonal-Round-Hexagonal. (Bolts and Nuts.)
X.P.M.	Expanded Metal.
Yeo.	Yellow (as 'yeo. deal').
∴	Therefore.

APPENDIX

Simple Systems You Can Make Yourself

1. MAIN LEDGER 'IN' PAGE

Cash books can be obtained cheaply and are suitable if you use one bank exclusively. Use left-hand pages for 'in' entries, and right-hand pages for 'out' payments.

DATE	DESCRIPTION	BANK A		BANK B	
JAN 2	Cash	180	50		
" 3	Cash / Cheques	275	00		
" 5	Cash / Cheques / P.O.			180	00
" 8	Cash	200	00		
" 8	Total Cr. Tr. Page 42	18	44		
" 10	Cash / Cheques	1,016	41		
" 15	Cash / P.Os			301	12

1   Main Ledger " In " Page

If you use more than one bank, or a bank and a Post-Office Giro account, then a page like that shown above is suitable. The item shown for January 8th. (Total Cr. Tr. page 42) is for use where customers pay your accounts by credit transfer. Each time you get a bank statement, total up the incoming credit transfers and enter them in this way, showing the bank statement page number as a reference.

2. MAIN LEDGER 'OUT' PAGE

You need a column for the name of the payee; the classification column is to help your accountant to analyse your expenditure which he does in order to produce your profit and loss account. If you have one bank, you will need two columns, one for bank cheques and one for cash. Otherwise you have to keep a separate book for cash payments. With two banks, as above, you would need three columns.

Very small items which are paid in cash can be entered in a petty cash book or voucher system, and the totals entered in the main ledger at intervals.

Wages and salaries, if paid in cash, need to be shown in the cash column, and an entry for 'cash' to pay the wages and other cash items, shown in the column of the appropriate bank.

Provided your P.A.Y.E. records are adequate, there may be no need to enter the amount paid to each individual in wages, the total is all that need be shown.

When you get the bank statement, you check it against this book and make sure that there are no mistakes such as other peoples' cheques being debited against your account, or credits missed.

3. SALES LEDGER

Lots of people are itching to sell you a sales ledger system, but here is one you can make for yourself. It is quite good enough for the new business to start with. You can duplicate the lines onto the sheets, or rule them yourself if you only have a few customers. You can clip them into a binder or file. Or you can buy them ready-printed at stationers.

Have a space at the top for the name and address of the customer; I leave room to write in branches if you deal with customers trading from more than one address on the same account. If you leave room also to put in discounts, terms, etc., or credit limit, then you can use the one ledger to keep all your information.

Date	Name	Classification	BANK A		BANK B		CASH	
Apr 4	C Nicholls	Printing	2,056	22				
" 5	Page Motors	Purchase of car	3,501	20				
" 6	A. Brown	Refund credit bal			29	11		
" 7	GPO	Telephones			102	20		
" 9	ECGD	Insurance			26	60		
" 12	Inland Revenue	PAYE/N.1.			482	90		
" 12	G.P.O.	Airmails					20	00
" 16	United Carriers	Delivery			46	60		
" 19	J. Smith	Royalty			48	39		
" 26	Borough Council	Rates			1,804	40		
" 27	Wessex N'papers	Advertising			66	00		
" 28	Cash				1,000	00		
" 29	Wages						906	20
" 29	Prideaux	Paper	5,619	23				
" 30	Bounced ch.				1	21		
" 30	SEEB	Electricity	183	29				
" 30	Total petty cash						62	09

2 Main Ledger "Out" Page

A.N. BROWN
48, NORTHGATE ST.,   Disc 35%
IPSWICH IP2 4EK

BRANCHES: HARWICH, ALDEBURGH, SAXMUNDHAM, BURY ST EDMOND

JAN 1	Harwich 7889	62	19				
" 4	Ipswich 7930	62	19				
" 16	Ipswich 8214	124	38				
" 21	Saxmundham 8404	17	72				
" 29	Aldeburgh 8800	108	31				
" 29	Bury 8801	62	19				
" 31	CREDIT Ipswich 1019 Faulties returned					6	62
" 31	Harwich 8990	62	19	Pd 27/2/..		492	55
FEB 1	Aldeburgh 9001	62	19				
" 16	Ipswich 9229	108	31				
" 26	Saxmundham 9440	108	31				
" 28	Ipswich 9604	124	38				

3   Sales Ledger Page

The third column from the left is for your invoice number or reference, which you quote on the statement monthly. Where a customer has several branches, as above, it helps also to record which Branch the invoice applies to. The first money column is for debits (invoices charged); in the second money column you can write date of payment, and the right-hand column is for credits and payments.

A good system is to draw a heavy line below items completely cleared (as has been done underneath Jan. 31 above). Items in the credit column should be written in red to save confusion.

Provided that V.A.T. has been properly shown on your invoices, it is not strictly necessary to show it separately again on your statement, and so the figures in your ledger should be the invoice totals, *including* V.A.T. where charged.

4. SUPER STOCK CONTROL SYSTEM

You can draw one of these up yourself and get it photocopied, or run it on a duplicator.

The left-hand column is for details of the item, the next is for the quantity to be stocked, the next four are for amendments to the stock quantity, and the 12 columns on the right are for the monthly stock checks. The bottom left of each square is for the quantity found to be in stock when it is checked, and the top right is for the quantity ordered.

Leave room at the top of the page for such things as discount terms and delivery time.

The example overleaf shows the story of the experience of a new business which sells widgets. In January, the widget representative calls and advises that straight and knurled widgets are the best sellers, knurled not quite as good as straight. The bevelled and reciprocating widgets are not so good. On this basis, the new trader, being cautious, orders 6 each of the 3 types of straight widget, and 3 each of the knurled. This, in fact, turned out not to be a very sensible order, but the advantage of a proper stock control system is that these errors are ironed out in the course of time and are not repeated.

The 4″ straight widget went quite well, and after a time our trader realised he could sell more than 6 in some months, so he changed the quantity and made stock up to 9 each month.

The 4″ knurled widget was rather a flop, and took until September to sell the first three. This is probably not really worth

J.H.S. Widgets (Sarum) Ltd.,
4 New St.,
Salisbury

Disc.: 30%
D/y: 1 week
19....

	Ref.	QTY	AMENDMENTS	JAN	FEB	MAR	APR	MAY	JUN	JUL	AUG	SEP	OCT	NOV	DEC
4" straight widget	HS 152	6	9	6/1	6/1	9/1	9/3	7/2	6/3	8/-	7/2	7/2			
4" knurled widget	HS 152K	3	1	3/1	3/3	1/3	1/3	1/2	1/2	1/-	1/-	1/1			
6" straight widget	HS 171	6	9 15 25	6/1	9/1	15/3	26/1	22/2	20/2	19/2	23/2	19/1			
6" knurled widget	HS 171K	3	9	3/1	6/1	5/1	6/1	6/1	5/3	8/1	6/2	6/1			
9" straight widget	HS 180	6	4 1	6/1	6/1	6/1	9/1	6/3	7/2	8/1	6/1	7/1			
9" knurled widget	HS 180K	3	R	3/1	3/-	3/-	3/-	3/4	3/1	3/-	3/-	R/2			
6" bevelled widget	HS 171B	6													
6" reciprocating widget	HS 171R	6	9				6/-	5/9	4/7	5/8	6/7	5/9			
Widget tool bit	HK 42	2					2/-	2/-	2/1	1/2	1/-	1/-			

4 Super Stock Control System

stocking, but our trader has decided to keep one, and replace it when sold, in order to offer a service to his customers.

The 6″ straight widget went very well indeed, so the stock quantity was put up to 9, then to 18, then to 25, and sales have stabilized at 20 a month. The 6″ knurled widget also went quite well, and the stock quantity was put up to 9 in April, as 6 had sold out twice.

9″ widgets were a complete flop. The straight variety took until September to sell 4, so is only worth keeping in singles, if that. The 9″ knurled did not sell at all, and in September our trader got permission to return his original three to the manufacturer for credit.

By April, it had become clear that demand was heavily concentrated in the 6″ range, so our trader decided to try both bevelled and reciprocating widgets in that length. These went well enough to be worth stocking, especially the reciprocating. There were also a few people asking for the tool kit, and it was found to be worth stocking a couple of these to meet this demand.

All this shows the advantage of stock control. An initial order for 27 widgets has turned to a regular monthly order of about four dozen! Intelligent analysis of the system has enabled our trader to maximize his profit from the high demand for 6″ straight widgets, to cut his stock and losses on the kinds which do not go, and to please his customers by always having in stock the widgets they want. The evidence of strong demand in the 6″ length led our trader to experiment with a wider variety of that kind, with extremely beneficial results.

You can see how much business would have been lost if our trader had waited for the representative to call again three months later, and then just re-ordered the same number of the lines which had gone.

5. EXAMPLE OF A CONTRACT OF EMPLOYMENT

In this statement under the Contracts of Employment Acts, XXX Company gives you, ... of
....
particulars of the terms and conditions on which it is employing you with effect from the ....

1. Your initial rate of pay is £........ per four-week month. You will be paid on the last Friday before April 5th each year and at four-weekly intervals thereafter.

2. Your normal hours of work are ...... per week. Your daily hours are ....
.... You are entitled to a one-hour mid-day meal break, 12.30 p.m. to 1.30 p.m. or at a different time by agreement.

3. In addition to Public Holidays and the other days on which the Office is closed at Christmas time, your holiday entitlement is two working weeks per calendar year. Dates are to be settled as far in advance as possible with the Manager. On completion of three years' service, you become entitled to an additional one working week's holiday per year, provided that this latter is taken during the Winter months October/April.

4. In addition, the Directors always give favourable consideration to requests for extra holidays without pay.

5. The Company will/will not continue to make up your normal pay during any unavoidable absence through sickness for at least one month, and for longer at its discretion.

Staff who have their pay made up in this way must furnish the necessary medical certificates and must claim health insurance in the event of absence through sickness for more than three consecutive days, and must repay to the Company all monies received from the D.H.S.S.

6. The Company does not provide a pension scheme.

7. You are entitled to receive one week's notice of termination after four weeks' employment; one week's notice for each year of continuous employment between two and twelve years, and twelve weeks' notice if the period of continuous employment is twelve years or more. You are required to give the Company one week's notice of termination, but longer if possible.

8. The title of your job is ....

9. *Disciplinary rules*: These are kept to the minimum, but the Company cannot employ those who break them.

(a) You are not allowed to enter the premises outside working hours.

(b) You are not allowed to smoke on the premises except in the Offices, and there only between 9.00 a.m. to 4.00 p.m.

(c) You are not allowed to use the Company's postage stamps for private purposes.

(d) You are not allowed to use the fire hose for any purpose except putting out a fire.

(e) You must ask the Manager's permission if you wish to:
   (1) make a private telephone call;

  (2) use the photocopier or duplicator or printer for private purposes;

  (3) purchase items of stationery, wrapping materials, etc.;

  (4) purchase stock;

and if permission is given, you must:

    (i) be as brief as possible on the 'phone;

  (ii) pay for calls made or materials used or bought, at cost;

(iii) do private work only during the lunch hour.

10. If at any time you are dissatisfied with any disciplinary decision affecting you, you may make a complaint to any of the Directors who are in the Office at the time.

11. If you have any individual grievance relating to your employment here, the procedure is for you to raise it with the Manager. If you are still dissatisfied, the procedure is then for you to raise the matter with any of the Company Directors who are in the Office at the time.

Note: In recent years British Governments have become very fond of tampering with employment legislation, and at the time of writing there is a proposal to make employers pay certain minimum sickness benefits, which could affect Clause 5. The up-to-date position should be checked, and leaflets are normally available from the Department of Employment.

INDEX

Accurate information for home and family in the

PAPERFRONTS

series

RIGHT WAY TO KEEP PONIES
RIGHT WAY TO KEEP DOGS
RIGHT WAY TO KEEP CATS
RIGHT WAY TO KEEP HAMSTERS
RIGHT WAY TO KEEP PET FISH
RIGHT WAY TO KEEP PET BIRDS
BABIES NAMES A–Z
DEEP FREEZE SECRETS
BASIC FREEZER RECIPES
HANDBOOK OF HERBS
RIGHT WAY TO MAKE JAMS

All uniform with this book

Elliot Right Way Books

BRIGHTON RD., LOWER KINGSWOOD,
SURREY U.K.

OUR PUBLISHING POLICY

HOW WE CHOOSE

Our policy is to consider every deserving manuscript and we can give special editorial help where an author is an authority on his subject but an inexperienced writer. We are rigorously selective in the choice of books we publish. We set the highest standards of editorial quality and accuracy. This means that a *Paperfront* is easy to understand and delightful to read. Where illustrations are necessary to convey points of detail, these are drawn up by a subject specialist artist from our panel.

HOW WE KEEP PRICES LOW

We aim for the big seller. This enables us to order enormous print runs and achieve the lowest price for you. Unfortunately, this means that you will not find in the *Paperfront* list any titles on obscure subjects of minority interest only. These could not be printed in large enough quantities to be sold for the low price at which we offer this series.

We sell almost all our *Paperfronts* at the same unit price. This saves a lot of fiddling about in our clerical departments and helps us to give you world-beating value. Under this system, the longer titles are offered at a price which we believe to be unmatched by any publisher in the world.

OUR DISTRIBUTION SYSTEM

Because of the competitive price, and the rapid turnover, *Paperfronts* are possibly the most profitable line a bookseller can handle. They are stocked by the best bookshops all over the world. It may be that your bookseller has run out of stock of a particular title. If so, he can order more from us at any time—we have a fine reputation for "same day" despatch, and we supply any order, however small (even a single copy), to any bookseller who has an account with us. We prefer you to buy from your bookseller, as this reminds him of the strong underlying public demand for *Paperfronts*. Members of the public who live in remote places, or who are housebound, or whose local bookseller is unco-operative, can order direct from us by post.

FREE

If you would like an up-to-date list of all paperfront titles currently available, send a stamped self-addressed envelope to
ELLIOT RIGHT WAY BOOKS, BRIGHTON RD.,
LOWER KINGSWOOD, SURREY, U.K.